To V

Good Wishes

Be Blessed

Mike

DIAMOND IN THE STONE

MY STORY AND POETRY

RIVER BLUE

BALBOA
PRESS
A DIVISION OF HAY HOUSE

Copyright © 2019 River Blue.

All rights reserved. No part of this book may be used or reproduced by any means, graphic, electronic, or mechanical, including photocopying, recording, taping or by any information storage retrieval system without the written permission of the author except in the case of brief quotations embodied in critical articles and reviews.

Scripture quotations marked KJV are from the Holy Bible, King James Version (Authorized Version). First published in 1611. Quoted from the KJV Classic Reference Bible, Copyright © 1983 by The Zondervan Corporation.

Balboa Press books may be ordered through booksellers or by contacting:

Balboa Press
A Division of Hay House
1663 Liberty Drive
Bloomington, IN 47403
www.balboapress.co.uk
1 (877) 407-4847

Because of the dynamic nature of the Internet, any web addresses or links contained in this book may have changed since publication and may no longer be valid. The views expressed in this work are solely those of the author and do not necessarily reflect the views of the publisher, and the publisher hereby disclaims any responsibility for them.

The author of this book does not dispense medical advice or prescribe the use of any technique as a form of treatment for physical, emotional, or medical problems without the advice of a physician, either directly or indirectly. The intent of the author is only to offer information of a general nature to help you in your quest for emotional and spiritual well-being. In the event you use any of the information in this book for yourself, which is your constitutional right, the author and the publisher assume no responsibility for your actions.

Any people depicted in stock imagery provided by Getty Images are models, and such images are being used for illustrative purposes only. Certain stock imagery © Getty Images.

Print information available on the last page.

ISBN: 978-1-9822-8081-9 (sc)
ISBN: 978-1-9822-8082-6 (e)

Balboa Press rev. date: 07/09/2019

CONTENTS

Dedication xi
Introduction xiii

MY STORY

Chapter 1   Childhood Memories 1
Chapter 2   Hunger and cold 6
Chapter 3   Taken.. 11
Chapter 4   Selected Amnesia 15
Chapter 5   Foster Care 17
Chapter 6   Foster Minus The Care 21
Chapter 7   Fear and More Fear 24
Chapter 8   Slow Learner 29
Chapter 9   Nightmares 31
Chapter 10   Escape to The Streets 33
Chapter 11   Probation Hostel 37
Chapter 12   Streets of London 42
Chapter 13   Approved School 46
Chapter 14   Detention Centre 49
Chapter 15   Borstal 53
Chapter 16   A Little Taste of Freedom 56
Chapter 17   Prison 59
Chapter 18   HMP Walton Blues 63
Chapter 19   HMP Faeces Parcels Galore 67

Chapter 20	"Slop Out"	69
Chapter 21	Becoming a Prison Baron	71
Chapter 22	Changes	75
Chapter 23	The Beginning of The End	77
Chapter 24	A Prayer Answered	82
Chapter 25	Searching	83
Chapter 26	I Found My Life and Future	86
Chapter 27	My Education	89
Chapter 28	A Nurse!	92
Chapter 29	My Arthur Daley Smart Suit	94
Chapter 30	Follow The Money	98
Chapter 31	Ambition	100
Chapter 32	Reaching for The Sky	102
Chapter 33	Money Rich Time Poor	103
Chapter 34	Searching	106
Chapter 35	Too Much to Bear	109
Chapter 36	The Path to My Enlightenment	110
Chapter 37	Meditation	112
Chapter 38	Dreams of Travel	114
Chapter 39	Meditation in India "it will pass"	125
Chapter 40	"It will Pass"	132
Chapter 41	Life's Lessons Hard Won	138

POETRY

Preface	147
Diamond in The Stone	151
The Journey to Awakening	154
In The Beginning	156
I Heard an Angels Voice	158
Seeking	160
"Change Going to Come"	162
Compulsive Thinking	164

Billy and Barney	166
Creating my Reality	168
Acceptance	170
Identity	172
Time	174
The Power Given to the Past	175
Wake up!	177
What is Now?	178
Detachment	179
Fear	180
Rising Sun	183
Comfort Zone	185
Snowfalls	187
Sleepless in the Night	189
Be "Now"	191
Here Now and Now is Gone	192
Become ye as a Little Child	194
Now in Silence	196
The Travelling Universe	198
Be the Watcher	201
Alchemy	202
Anger	203
Attachments	205
Mystery of Fear	207
What are Lies	210
The World Within	211
The Human Body	215
The Effects of Unseen Energies	220
Energy of the Trees	221
The Mind	222
Spark of Life	223
Human Mind Insanity	224
The Earth Trembles	226
The Journey	227

Let the Past Go	228
Waiting	229
The Mind Trap	230
"Me" "I" and "Mine"	231
Only Now is Real	232
I'm Late!	233
Captain Speaking	234
Arrival in Paradise	236
A New Day	238
Out of Body Journeys	239
The Higher Self	241
The Master	243
Magic	245
Prison Planet Earth	247
The Connection	250
Life Surrounds all Things!	252
My Special Friend	255
When Death comes Calling	256
Locked in Time	257
Hidden Energies	258
A Body of Flesh	259
The Brain	261
Satori	263
The Secret	264
Imprisoned by the Mind	266
Once Upon a Stone!	268
Impossible Life	270
Living Power	274
No Time	275
Creating Gaps	276
Like Jesus and The Buddha	277
Awaken	278
I Awoke and Declared Freedom	279
Being Love	280

Unique R U 281
Say "Goodbye" to You 282
The Imposter called "Ego" 283
Daffodils 285
Apple Tree 286
A Young Prisoners Tale 287
The Swamp 288
The Event 291
He Cried! 293
Don't Strive after the Wind 295
No Resistance 296
Addictions 297
"Know ye Not that ye are Gods"? 298
No More Separation 299
"My Father and your Father" 300
Windows 302
He Healed Me! 305
King Queen Villain and Thief 308
Experiencing Your Awakening signs 311

DEDICATION

Dedicated to all who gave me encouragement, with this support I found a sense of personal worth and value. My homeless companions who taught me that even homeless I could survive, showing me the warmest and safest spots to sleep in the City Streets. I survived, some of you did not! "Thank you" Angels of the night who had tougher lives than mine, you took me in sharing what little you had with someone who had less. The companions who taught me the survival skills of life in various institutions Remand Homes, Detention Centre, Borstal where I also learned some business skills too! Some of you didn't make it! But it may be true to say, "I survived because of you". Thanks to those employed in the Justice System who really did care and tried to help me find my way, your employment was my school of hard knocks, where we in your care watched each other's backs, fought together and sometimes each other! For my Church friends… for your support as I struggled to gain a sense of value and self-respect. I learned to trust again and without you my life may have turned out very differently. Thank you, Mr B, down under for your guidance taking a chance and trusting me. Barbara my friend mentor and guide whom I will never forget, your kindness and for making me part of your family "I was a stranger and you took me in" When I failed at exams losing my confidence, you gently lovingly guided encouraged and helped me succeed "thank you".

My children

I am proud of you all and love you. My story may give you a better understanding of your own journey. I hope it gives you courage to pursue your dreams regardless of circumstances. Your journey has just begun. You will find your way with many happy memories and wonderful stories to tell your children. It took me awhile to banish my demons to take back the power from circumstances. Don't allow your mind to be your master, be the master of your mind! Train your mind to find the love in all people in all things. Most importantly without ego truly love yourselves. Do not fear anything or anyone, fear is a powerful force that can stop you doing so many wonderful things. Continue to give your hearts to love and the wonders of life will fill your being.

INTRODUCTION

A Life Worth Living

This is my story of another life lived. A life of contrasting circumstances. Starving Wealthy Poor Homeless Street Fighter Loneliness Learning Difficulties Prisoner Loved Unloved. From an uneducated lost soul to a caring compassionate human being Nurse Trainer Teacher Property Developer Business Manager International Business Manager Sunday school Teacher World Traveller Business Owner. More importantly than all "things" I have learned the purpose of life is "love" and oneness with all. Non-judgement is a hard lesson to learn with many challenges but the rewards of success are many!

Being without a positive role model from day one I had no direction or purpose. I crawled out of the streets of Liverpool at age 19 Psychologically physically beaten and scarred. I survived neglect and abuse of body mind and spirit. I left my circumstances with a blind determination never to return to the life I was leaving behind. I did not know how hard the journey would be as memories of childhood trauma are not easily shaken or forgotten.

In the darkness of the subconscious the hurts wait to reveal themselves as emotional pain fear anger and hopelessness. The pain wants to be set free like a caged lion restlessly pacing to and fro. My struggle to break away and find a life worth living has been a daily battle to tame the lions! As a child I was delivered into a Care System that didn't care! Who further neglected and rejected and abused by those assigned by the courts to protect and nurture me. I did find a life worth living after struggling with a mind filled to bursting with conditioned negative beliefs and painful memories. Escaping the abusers, I recognised my thoughts and emotions were my opposition to finding a life worth living. Life has been an incredible adventure and I intend that it will always be so. I have learned one lesson well; it is that Life Is Worth Living! It is a short time that goes by fast. I will continue to make the most of this short time. I hope you reading my words can imagine yourselves in my shoes it's the only way another's life can be understood.

It has taken tremendous effort and courage to build a life worth living to find meaning and reclaim personal value and self-love. I once thought of destroying myself but chose to destroy my self-limiting beliefs and conditioned sense of worthlessness instead! My journey led me to the pain of the abandoned child, the adolescent and young adult. I chose to relive it all by re-entering the darkness of my subconscious mind and was rewarded with understanding forgiveness and healing. I hugged listened to and reassured the child as we relived the pain together, we talked about how loving and loved he was by me and the universe. And like the sun dissolving the clouds my childhood pain became something more beautiful… I visited and befriended my tough lonely adolescent and young adult, we talked listened and cried together as we felt our pain, then said goodbye with deep love affection and gratitude.

My existence began with parents who found the circumstances of their lives hard to bear. They tried their best but lost direction as we all do sometimes! Alcohol and prescription drugs played a large part in my parent's struggle. I'm grateful for my parent's efforts and for giving me life. Their lives too were tremendously difficult and have now passed on to a better existence. My resentment and anger of being rejected was hard to shake for many years. The tough sometimes violent slums of Liverpool schooled me well for what was to come.

My time in Foster Homes Remand Centres Young offender's institutions Detention Centre Borstal and Prisons nearly destroyed my belief in myself and humanity, but also taught me what I did not want from life! Since then I have lived and worked amongst the Rich Poor Sick Dying Homeless Addicted the Imprisoned Educated and not so educated, and each gave me priceless tours of their worlds! Life is the school master but all lessons come at a cost! A big lesson I had to learn was "judge not"! Maybe you reading my words are on a similar journey as mine? Feeling as I did on occasion "I can't do this, it will be easier to go back" get lost in the sea of other lost souls. To you I say "make tomorrow a better day; the future is what you have the will to make it and you are not alone"! I nearly gave up until I believed something better was ahead and there always has been!

At age 20 feeling lost I called out in my darkest hour not knowing if any higher power really existed. I had heard God mentioned along the way but this was my first cry for help. I was tired of living. In a darkened room I was about to jump, I didn't care, I wanted to jump! I wanted to be gone forever! I felt my life wasn't worth living. I received an answer to that prayer! A light lit up the darkness I felt inside. Something on that desperate night heard and felt my pain and a message was delivered straight to my heart.

The answer was overwhelming and saved my life! I had made up my mind to leave the world but that answer came to me not in words; no voice was heard or angel seen! But my whole being was filled with what I can only describe as light! a sense of awe and wonder at came from somewhere? I had been given a feeling of being reborn for the first time! And again I say "Thank You" to whoever or whatever felt my pain and assisted me! The answer was so real that I began a journey of self-discovery which is not for the closed minded, but for those truly willing and ready to explore the world of possibilities.

MY STORY

CHAPTER 1

Childhood Memories

I was one of 9 children born in Liverpool. I was the fourth oldest. Can't ever remember being together as a family for any length of time. We would meet up in different Foster homes or institutions as we got older. We were each a part of the other but on our own individual journey! Memories of Mum Dad brothers and sisters are few. Mom and Dad would go missing sometimes not returning at all, leaving us to fend for ourselves. In one house I remember in Norris Green Liverpool my brothers and sisters and I were taken away by police and social services to various Foster Homes after authorities were alerted by street neighbours of the dirty hungry children roaming the streets asking neighbours for food!

Several times my instinct led me to hide away on such occasions, and I would find myself alone hungry cold and confused. On one such day after my sisters and brothers were taken I found myself alone in an empty house. I must have been a sight, a skinny kid with a squint, one eye in Birkenhead the other in Manchester! and two prominent goofy front teeth! When I spoke to another person in my thick Liverpool scouse accent, they'd look behind them wondering if I was speaking to them or someone else as the right eye always looked in a different direction to my left eye! My hair cut by the Liverpool Training Centre for barbers for free was always unevenly cut! At this Barber Centre the Lice (nits) would crawl on and around the gown, two nits side by side was a race! A brown woollen short sleeved jumper grey socks pulled to my knees and plastic pink sandals seemed to be my only outfit. I always felt cold and hungry and the day my Brothers and Sisters were taken away by Social Services was no exception.

No food had been in the house since mom had left days before and the house was in darkness. There was no electric and as evening fell the street lights appeared ghostly through the dirty net curtains hanging from loose string. The electricity and gas was turned off by Suppliers for failure to pay outstanding bills. Yellowy brown linoleum covered the floor, in places much was missing as we had ripped it up to light a fire on the cold alone days. We burned anything for warmth and light i.e. the flooring our clothes the wallpaper doors cupboards anything to keep warm. This day I had hidden in the bushes and watched the other children be taken away. I never knew if Mom or Dad would ever come back. Afterwards I knocked on the neighbour's doors asking for food drink and money for the Electric and Gas meters.

I have wished I could have been born into a home filled with enough of everything and memories of wonderful times. I don't remember toys cuddles or affection, being tucked into bed at night or going for long walks, having a book read to me! How different it could have been. When others tell stories of happy family time I know I missed something important!

I was born in 1953 and the streets of Liverpool where my playground. The scars of the Second World War could be seen with bombed scorched black buildings, piles of brick rubble and stench of damp charred decaying wood. Liverpool City Centre and Docks appeared bleak and dark and were the slum playgrounds for all the ragged children of the neighbourhood. As a boy I remember street gangs of children like packs of dogs claiming certain buildings and areas as their territory. Any kids who trespassed would get verbally abused humiliated and often physically beaten! As a boy I learned to fight! Learning "the bigger they were the harder they would fall"! I got pretty good at it and eventually other kids left me alone. I became one of the pack and only those who didn't know me ever challenged me. I was always on my guard and ready. A disrespectful look or word that's all it took, and Id unleash a swift rebuke. In my youth and early years, I learned to be quick and never broadcast my intention making it too late for the challenger to come back at me! My small size and speed was my strength and they were always surprised! When I met someone who had learned in the same streets I would meet my match! Afterwards we usually ended up friends out of respect for the other's toughness.

Street language was the norm "F.. k this F..k that C..t Tw.t Bas…d" every slum word was used as every day vocabulary! We learned from the streets and slum life was our reality and Teacher. The more you swore the tougher you appeared and the tougher you appeared the less you were victimised! The cobbled streets demolished houses stench of faeces stale urine and rat infested buildings where everywhere. Steel tram lines running through cobbled streets from an earlier time could be seen all over Liverpool as Tarmac had not yet covered every surface of the UK! The new Cathedral nicknamed affectionately "Paddy's Wigwam" was only half completed after years and millions of pounds being spent, delayed by the commencement of the Second World War. Later completed the New Cathedral stands out on the horizon and can be seen for miles. The wise powers thought a 2nd Cathedral was needed for the countless struggling hungry poverty stricken families of Liverpool! But it neither provided Food Shelter or warmth to the millions whose quality of life was less than the Bishops and Priests! I climbed broken walls of bombed buildings the bricks and wood my toys. Hands knees torn dirty clothing were the results of my search for treasure which never appeared! The thought of finding treasure excited me as a child, my make believe world far from the misery of poverty which families endured then and today!

My world was dirty grey and depressingly dark. Poverty has a definite feel and odour to it. Food was always scarce and being able to afford anything was the problem. Hunger constantly rumbling in my stomach growling and complaining noisily. As a boy I would make my way to the kitchen bins refuge areas behind local Cafés Restaurants and Hotels around the City Centre to scavenge for food. I would find cooked chicken carcasses discarded as being of no more use to the customers and chef, they always had lots of chicken meat still on the bones and tasted delicious!

I was a regular at the bins and occasionally a kind staff member would wrap the leftovers for me. Chicken carcases became so popular with the local people later on that restaurants began to sell each carcass for one penny and later a shilling for several. I remember a time I'd arrived back to my grandmother's home, it being a flat in the Bullring in Liverpool where my mom lived with her mom for a while. Getting there with the chicken scraps I was greeted like a little hero, which made me feel proud and important. It would be many years before I would feel proud and important again… many years!

The chicken scraps tasted like a feast. By pulling the wish bone we believed that if we got the larger piece of bone on pulling it apart with our little finger our wishes would come true! I accepted all without question. I had nothing to compare my life to it was as it was. My wishes never came true even when I got the large side of the wishbone! What did I wish for? I can only imagine I wished for a warm home where I could feel safe with more chicken! Aloneness became normal! Many years would pass before I would feel I belonged anywhere. I never spoke of my feelings because nobody asked! The emotional emptiness followed me like a dark shadow. I felt disconnected from everything and everyone with anger and sadness bubbling just below the surface. The wall around me got higher and higher then one day I just didn't speak anymore cocooned in empty nothingness!

I realised Father Christmas was someone who didn't like going into the slummier areas of Liverpool and wish bones never made wishes come true! I had an Uncle (Uncle Hughie) mums Brother I was told, who made his living from playing the mouth organ and tying himself into a sack with chains and escaping like Houdini, then collecting money from the crowds who would gather around him and clap him for his effort and entertainment.

Aunty Mary, mum's Sister died young she was very kind I remember. Aunty Mary sold sticks of Liverpool rock to the people getting off the ferries boats coming from across the Mersey River at the Pier Head Docks land area. When she died, not sure of what? her body was laid in a coffin and was displayed in the house of my grandmother. I remember pulling myself up on tip toe nervously to see into the brown varnished wooden coffin. Plastic imitation copper handles gave the coffin an expensive appearance. Aunty Mary looked very peaceful and beautiful to my little mind. Her body was draped in sets of Catholic Rosary beads and prayer books. White silk sheeting and a gown frilled at the neck covered the lower and upper portion of her body. Her beautiful angelic face looked peaceful hands clasped in prayer and she looked like an Angel. I thought she would wake up at any moment and was buried alongside many other young men boys and children sacrificed to poverty never to fulfil their dreams! My memory has always been of a young beautiful and loving person who for reasons I cannot remember? I miss her. She must have been nice because there was a big party with lots of people drinking getting merry beside the coffin for several evenings, all saying how nice Mary had been, drinking to her passing which didn't make too much sense to me at the time.

CHAPTER 2

Hunger and cold

I was fourth in a line of nine children, we had all been born one year apart, which gives understanding to why mum and dad were so stressed and unable to take care of the children they loved. I recall several houses I had lived in all cold damp and always lacking in food, all with a sense of misery and poverty about them. Council houses in slum areas where all the same in appearance with dull green gloss paint on every window frame and door. Linoleum was a standard feature of Government provided houses. Central heating had not yet arrived in early 1950's so heating was about coal or anything you could find to burn in the fireplace.

As a boy I would go find old wood at bombed derelict houses where I played and drag it back to burn. Our cupboard doors garden fencing linoleum and newspapers enabled us to stay warm for a while in the cold winter months. Bedroom windows in winter time would be covered in a thin cold sheet of ice and hanging icicles, old coats and several children in a bed kept us warm. A game we played was to scratch with a finger nail noughts and crosses on the iced window panes or draw picture scenes that appeared in the magic of my imagination. As the ice melted pools of water gathered on the rough painted window ledges and dripped down the walls. Mould mildew always on faded damp wallpaper which got so wet it peeled away and hung from the dark stained walls. The grey green black mould

Diamond in the Stone

grew on ceilings and every corner. I did try to childishly decorate the bedroom wall with a Batman sign drawn with thick tipped black indelible ink marker pen, for which I got clobbered but still remember my drawing with pride to this day.

Blankets and bed clothes were scarce 4-5 children of varying ages with old and damp coats for blankets! The fleas constantly biting leaving itchy red blotches did not make for a good night's sleep! I didn't know this was poverty at the time so never complained. First up was best dressed was the norm for everyone. My body was always itching and I considered the fleas as pets finding fleas and searching each other's hair for head lice was fun that is until my hair was combed with a shiny hard steel nit comb! The comb had teeth like a row of sharpened needles, it scratched my scalp and tore at my hair leaving my head very sore afterwards. When a nit was combed out I would push down on it with a thumbnail resulting in a satisfying loud crack! The local school "Nit Nurse" supplied head lice killer this smelly head lice lotion left my hair shining greasy and smelling of disinfectant. The smell singled me out by other kids who knew I had nits (head lice). Name calling would follow and ended in me fighting the name callers as I tried to regain my dignity.

Scurvy and body scabs were treated with a chalky pink chemical smelling cream that stung my eyes and testicles (Calamine Lotion) it dried a powdery white on the skin making me look like a zombie child and I dreaded its application and name calling at School followed! The toilet in one house was at the bottom of the garden built of red brick with grey tiled roof, had a wooden door of tongue and groove painted corporation green. Going to the end of the garden down a flagged weed covered pathway on a cold night or day, was a horrible but unavoidable. I wiped my bottom with old bits of damp Liverpool Echo Newspaper, there was no wash basin for hand washing.

My arse was always itching constantly from the printing ink and newspaper left sticking to it. Inside the loo bowl was black stinking of urine and faeces. I was always glad to get out of it. I did note

River Blue

looking back that many of the kids in the neighbourhood could be seen scratching their arses too and had shiny smelly heads!

More often than not there was no food in any of the dirty flaking battered green painted cupboards. A cupboard door was often missing taken off used for firewood. Being hungry mum and dad missing, I went out one night and using a wire coat hanger which I stretched out straight, keeping the hook on the end. I made my way to the shops where I had would try get something to eat. I waited on the corner looking out for passers-by in case they suspected what I was up to.

My small hand and arm fitted easily through the shop letterbox positioned at floor level. I fed the wire through the letter box of the Grocery Shop extending my arm as far into the shop as possible, and with the wire hook pulled the on Wheels Wrack of "Knorr Packet Soups towards the letterbox and pulled the Soup Wrack onto the floor carefully guiding each packet of soup towards the letterbox getting as many packets as possible through the letterbox. On returning home, the house was in darkness and cold, the Electric was off. I boiled water in an old kettle over a make shift newspaper fire in the hearth. The noodle soup was my favourite; it was a feast and it felt like a party as we huddled around the fire with our hot soup as the dancing flames of the fire flickered shadows of light across peeling wallpaper. It was a good day and we slept wrapped in each other, covered in coats our clothing still on.

I found myself alone on several occasions and was always scared. With no lighting or heating, the greedy Electric Meter constantly demanded shilling coins. I managed at one time, to file down the edge of a half-penny on the bare larder concrete shelf then fed the coin into the meter which worked a treat. When no half penny was available it was scary in the dark alone. The Electricity Coin Meter man would come to empty the meter and find the steel box full of filed down half pennies!

Winter times were extremely cold so one night we dug a hole through to next doors concrete coal bunker and shovelled the coal from their bunker then made a fire to stay warm. When the neighbour discovered it all hell broke loose, and again we suffered the cold in silent. At weekends we had Government Dinner Tickets issued by Social Services which allowed us a school meal for free. There were vegetables real meat and a pudding! I looked forward to going for those meals leaving with a full stomach and satisfied. It was a special occasion giving a sense of living to what I now know was a miserable existence!

On another hungry occasion I headed to a local farm where vegetables were grown Potatoes, Cabbages Beetroots and a Tomato Green House. I had set my sights on stealing some Potatoes. I climbed the fence in the early evening and made my way to the Potato patch, keeping low so not to be seen and began digging and scraping up great big potatoes they appeared that way to my 8-year-old mind. Lost in my digging imagining how nice these potatoes where going to taste, I was suddenly without warning scooped up by very strong rough thick skinned hairy hands. I went limp with terror dropping the potatoes. I was turned to face my imagined monster, he was about 60 something, short stubby strong body, wrinkled hard looking facial skin unshaven.

He held me at his chest height at arm's length, my feet dangling in mid-air. I screamed loudly, the man ignoring my cries to let me go, carried me to a nearby shed pushed me in, the wooden door slamming behind him. I heard a bolt being applied on his side. Then he called into me "you little bastard, sick of you fuckers stealing my crops, you will stay there until the police come for you" heavy footsteps faded into the distance then silence and sobbing of a scared child…

I was in total darkness in the shed and couldn't move for fear. I wet myself, the pee ran down the inside to the outside of my short grey pants, down my leg and I began to feel cold. I was thinking "I was a prisoner that he was going to kill me and bury my body in his allotment" Crying in the darkness I could hear scuttling and scratching in the shed, after what seemed eternity in the darkness I heard the heavy footsteps returning. The bolt was pulled back from the door, the door flung open with a crash that left me shaking.

Silhouetted in the doorway against a background of a moonlit night was the booted man. I screamed terrified expecting to be killed.

The man came towards me, telling me in a soft voice, "ok that's enough little mister spud stealer, this time I am letting you go, but next time it's the Police do you understand, and tell ye mates" he pointed to the door and that's all it took. I was off like a whippet and ran as fast as my legs would go heart pounding in my chest like it was going to explode. I felt relieved that I had escaped and never stopped running until I reached our empty house. I had hungry nightmares for nights afterwards. I never told anybody until now about my hungry adventure as it would have attracted possible punishment, even at a young age we were told "never involve Police" they were not to be trusted!

CHAPTER 3

Taken

Mum and dad screamed and shouted at each other constantly viciously and physical fighting always followed. We would scream and cry in terror then Police and Social Services followed. Doors slammed, furniture and any object became missiles and weapons. Id cower in corners hands over my ears, curled up under beds and tables where ever it felt safe during these fights between my parents. I have since learned that both mum and dad were on many GP Prescribed Drugs. Diazepam Purple Hearts. Tablets for sleep tablets for depression and many various others that were freely prescribed in the 60s. Alcohol and gambling were major contributors to the family's demise. Dad was a returned Army Veteran. I am told that he fought in the battles in Burma and received the Burma Star awarded for bravery. Many soldiers who survived those battles carried my Fathers the Coffin that was draped in a Union Jack Flag on the day of his funeral. Dad was also arrested for being drunk and disorderly, but allowed to go free after the Police would found his Medal for Bravery the "Burma Star". Dad was an amateur Army trained Boxer I was told. I witnessed him on several occasions literally knock out several burley men.

I was also knocked out by him after challenging him at age 16 to fight. I had gotten drunk and wanted to beat him, but seconds after my words I was out cold! I didn't even see it coming. Afterwards he laid me on the settee were I found myself on awakening with a sore jaw. Dad died alone after laying dead for several days in an empty flat. Mum lived 100 yards away but they hadn't spoken to each other in a while I was told. He died of a massive Oesophageal Haemorrhage and bled to death.

At age 20 after leaving Liverpool I travelled back from Birmingham to see him several weeks before his death. I wanted to try and establish some sort of communication that would allow me to know him better and he to get to know me. But on the day he remained distant and uncommunicative. I left feeling disappointed. So to the end, I never knew him, and he didn't know me. I wish things would have been different but sadly things were as they were, the only thing I could change was me. When he died I cried a lot but I didn't know why? Maybe lost opportunities?

A memory of my Dad……Screams and shouting, Dad holding a bloody hand to his chest trying to stop the blood spurting from a stab wound to his hand, Mum screaming obscenities, hands to my ears shaking in fear. I wanted to disappear curled up behind a chair. Dad leaving shouting in blood soaked clothing, Mum screaming.

A memory … I'm a skinny small boy 9 years old, in a Foster Home ordered to remain in a cold white bare room in fear of a threatened punishment. For 8yrs my food being passed to me through a small square hole in the wall. Ordered not to speak. Eating the same food in silence each and every day for eight years. I hate Pearl Barley soup with a vengeance. Social Services would visit and for an hour and life changed! When Official Visitors arrived I would be given toys, food became edible and normal and I was allowed to leave the dining room! When Social Services visited I would be asked to sit in the Foster families "Aunties lounge"! And instructed to go to the forbidden playroom full of toys! When the Inspection Visitors left all returned to normal, toys were taken away and the silence of the Dining Room!

My first memory of being taken away from my parents became a nightmare for years! 8years old hiding behind a privet bush knees scraped hole in my dirty short pants, two odd socks and plastic sandals hiding afraid and watching. I had turned the corner to the house on a street a mile long with similar red brick corporation houses all doors painted green with junk in the overgrown gardens, wrecked cars bikes smashed crockery bags of rubbish tyres bottles and various other rubbish.

I had noticed a large White Van like a School Bus parked outside the house. I hesitated to go further, seeing a man with shirt and tie was unusual and I felt scared. Another man and a woman were sitting in the van. My Brothers and Sisters were being escorted out of the front door towards the waiting Van. I noticed the Van was not empty some Brothers and Sisters were already captured. They looked scared crying and looking towards the house. I knew I must not be seen or get into that Van! I stayed hidden watching as the van drove away not knowing where they were going? I only knew my Brothers and Sisters were taken away by strangers in smart suits and ties. I don't know how long I stayed behind the hedge it felt forever. I was cold and scared but waited until the sky grew darker. I was afraid to move in case they came back for me.

Eventually I walked shivering and scared towards the house. I knocked on the front door, nobody answered, I looked through the letter box but could see nothing just darkness. I stretched up to the window trying to see inside, it was darkness inside too. I went through the green rotting wood gate into the back garden, the back door was locked! I went next door and knocked, I looked up at a woman with a faded flowered apron wrapped around her stout hips, rollers in her hair and cotton scarf tied over the rollers. She knew me and stated "your mom has left" "where"? I asked, "I don't know" she spoke kindly in a broad Liverpool accent and asked me if I "wanted to come in"? "no" and ran as fast as I could towards the end of the street turned the corner and kept running through the darkness in the direction of a Bus Stop.

I remembered my Mom's Mother "ninny smith" we called her. I remembered roughly where she lived in the Centre of Liverpool a place they called the "Bullring" near the new Cathedral. The Bullring was a circle of Corporation flats on three levels, it had at that time a reputation for being a place strangers did not enter.

River Blue

I had decided to catch a bus but I had no money. I spotted a Bus; I thought it would take me to the City. I got on and sat down. The Ticket man came towards me with his metal ticket machine and leather money bag strapped across his chest and asked "where you going"? I told him I was trying to find my Mum, he asked "where is she then"? "The Bullring" I replied, "I've got no money" he looked at me, he was going to ask me to get off the bus, but he didn't! He stared at me awhile and said "ok lad I will let you know when we get there"!

I sat quietly on the bus not knowing where Mom Dad or Brothers and Sisters had gone. I was a small boy dirty face grey socks eyes red from crying, travelling alone looking out of the window watching but not seeing...it was warm on the bus. I was feeling lost hungry tired and alone. The Busman called me after forever and said "here we are" and let me off the bus. It was dark but the street lights of Liverpool City lit up my way. I tried hard to remember how to get to my Grandma's house, getting lost up this street and that. Until after much knocking on random doors, a neighbour told me there was a lady that sounded like my ninny smith just two doors away.

I ran through the dark scared and knocked on a familiar looking door. My Grandma answered the knock, she was about 80yrs old small with papery dry looking pale skin, which hung in places like it was loose. Grey hair pulled tightly to the back of her head into a bun a thin dark ribbon tied around it.

She smelt of tobacco snuff powder and stale urine, wearing a long cotton black dress and a faded flowered apron covering her waist. Two brown snuff powder streaks run from her bony nose to her wrinkled lips. She knew me and her dark sunken eyes looked me up and down, smiling a toothless smile she asked me to come in, "ye mom's inside come in son". Mom was there drunk and she slurred, "You know you can't stay, we have nowhere to live"! Later a car with smartly dressed man and a lady asked me to go with them. I later learned mom and Dad had been evicted Brother's Sisters taken into care sent to several different Foster Homes.

CHAPTER 4

Selected Amnesia

I had grown up feeling totally alone. By age 17 I had blanked my childhood out. I couldn't remember anything of the many foster homes, the abuse names or places, I had buried them all with myself. Selective amnesia remained with me for many years into adulthood.

I couldn't understand, why I could not remember. But thanks to a Paul McKenna's Self-Hypnosis cassette entitled "Recovering lost Memories" my memories slowly returned. I played it each night in bed for several weeks whilst going off to sleep. I had tried up to this point very hard to remember my childhood unsuccessfully always wondering why it was missing. My teens years were troubled I could not feel happiness or the joy of living. My moods swung from low to empty depressed states.

I would become angry for the smallest of provocations, it was to be a daily battle for many years to come. I worked hard to keep busy as being busy left little room for morose or depressed feelings. I had a fear of sleeping from age 14 to 30 haunted by the same nightmare, followed by sleep paralysis. In this nightmare I would be descending a dark hallway, making my way down dark damp smelly stairs. I could feel cold spider webs, the wet slime on the walls as I felt my way slowly down. I would hear scuttling sounds of unknown creatures in the darkness, in the dream I knew that at the bottom would be something or someone evil and terrifying, at the point I had descended the last step, I would awake sweating and paralysed literally with fear and dread. Not able to move or breath trying to scream, trying to breath would last several minutes fearing I was going to die! Then finally taking a deep long breath with relief covered in cold sweat.

Not wanting to sleep would see me wandering about at night until early hours. I would do this each night until I was so exhausted, then on getting into bed Id fall fast asleep. When the lost memories started coming back to me I remembered the younger years of family violence the care homes and how isolated I felt.

CHAPTER 5

Foster Care

Several institutional children's homes came back to my memory. Each except had one thing in common, they did not care! It was the 1960's, the Beatles songs where heard being played everywhere. Hey Jude. Sergeant Peppers. Ticket to ride. Penny Lane, their music was part of the world around me. I had no access to Radio, TV or music as the Foster home didn't allow it until aged 14 when I began to abscond. The Beatles could be heard in café bars, schools, on the streets, all over, even as a child their music made me feel good.

My first memory of being in care, was in a Nuns Convent, the Nuns in black and grey abbots holding rosary beads, heads down, whispering prayers from twittering lips, walking quick little steps along cold grey paved floors of the convent building. I could hear these steps constantly, the sounds of footsteps echoing with hollowness on the flat plain stone floors.

A bell would ring at the same hours every day, calling us all to Mass in the chapel. Mass would be led by a small Irish Catholic priest. None of the Nuns were like Julie Andrews, they appeared sullen and where very strict. Every minute of the day went like clockwork, if I was late god forbid, and I often was, getting out of bed at 6:30 am each morning. I had to wash dress make my bed, tidy my dormitory space, get breakfast served by the Nuns. Our job was to set the long brown wooden rough tables with dishes cups cutlery and drinking glasses.

After breakfast the bell would sound, all would become quiet, off we would all go to mass in a cold stone Chapel. The Chapel was decorated in colourful paintings of the Stations of the Cross, depicting the tortures of Jesus, his scourging and crucifixion fascinated me. Large glazed decorated stone floor tiles. Several tall statues of Jesus, St Francis and other Saints painted gold and bright colours stood appearing to watch every move I made.

The Alter was made of carved stone, with white laced cotton covering the whole alter. A yellow metal cross stood proudly in the middle of the Alter as a reminder of the torture instrument used to kill Jesus, gleaming and polished! If my son was killed would I want the dagger or gun kept on display and polish it each day? It did not make sense to me. I believe the history of Jesus, but I find this concept difficult! Always there where fresh flowers placed there by the nuns each day. If late for mass, all the Nuns eyes would turn on you, you would feel that God would punish you. This punishment often came from Mother Superior with a flat ruler across the hand or back of legs, it really stung. I was ordered to attend early morning mass with the nuns every morning, like it or not, I did not argue, for fear of Gods, and mother superiors' punishment. Where was the kindness and affection? It was more about the rules doctrine and rituals! I learned about Christ but saw no evidence of Christ like behaviour!

After Mass, we, that is six sometimes more Children of varying ages, one being my older Brother Tony had to work on the farm. We attended schooling in between work assignments. My brother Tony was about aged 10 we never knew were our Brothers and Sisters where at that time. The event that stands out here, is my brother putting a pitch fork through his foot while we were mucking out soiled straw from the barn floor, otherwise my recall is limited other than its strict routine.

In the convent I didn't feel harmed in any way, talking was forbidden except in exceptional circumstances and allocated areas. I enjoyed it most of all at bed times, were we would whisper as quietly as possible to each other, a nun assigned, would sit outside the dormitory on a small wooden chair all night to watch over us, but she often would fall asleep, we would sneak past her snoring head to get to the toilet without waking her, for fear of her waking, and getting the ruler as punishment.

I cannot remember how long we stayed there for, but one-day mum turned up in a car driven by a Social worker, telling us she had been given a council house and we were going home. That day was a happy day but not many weeks after it was back to another care home!

At age 9 years old I was picked up in Liverpool city centre caught shoplifting in TJ Hughes department store. The police were called they tried unsuccessful to contact my parents. Social services took me to a temporary children's home in the Wooten area of Liverpool for 4-5 weeks. The home had 20 other children some teenagers. It was strictly run by men in suits and ties, who ensured order and stopped the occasional fight and other misdeeds.

The home was clean, we were well fed, assisted in every way the men who ran it did so with kindness towards the children in their care. Then one day I was escorted out with several Social workers to a court building, I was made legally a ward of the court for my care and protection. Bewildered frightened and confused, I didn't understand why I couldn't be with my parents. I was in a daze numb, didn't know what, or how to react, not knowing what was happening. A white van with suited escorts took with me, and several of my brothers and sisters, to a Foster Home in Liverpool where I spent the next 8 years!

The Foster Home we arrived at was in a long street of tidy well-kept houses, the one we arrived at was 2 council houses converted into one, so as to accommodate both the foster family and up to 7 fostered children. This foster family was made up of the father Mr B and mother Mrs B and two sons. On arrival there with Social Services we were shown immediately about the house by Mrs B (Aunty) she smiled a lot while the Social Services were with us, after Social Services left, we were given our orders and the smiles ceased!

We were told that we must always call them Auntie and Uncle! Never speak to the Sons, never go into their side of the house, which was everywhere but the dining room! We were to always stay in the dining room! If we wanted the Toilet we should call from the dining room, and wait until permission was granted. We were informed all meals would be served through a hatch into the white painted dining room wall and never go into any other areas! We were scared from day one of this woman, she was about 45 stern looking, she seldom smiled except when Official Visitors were about, which turned out to be not very often! The two sons A age 10 a small dumpy blond lad who attended a private school for boys appeared to be sneering whenever eye contact was made. K age 20 was tall slim and spoke not at all. They appeared spoilt aloof and never spoke to us ever!

CHAPTER 6

Foster Minus The Care

The foster Uncle was tall pale with gaunt features and small grey eyes, grey haired about 40. He never spoke much; we didn't see much of him ever. He worked as a security guard and often brought home his German shepherd...a fierce looking unfriendly brown and black furred dog.

Social Services inspectors came to the Foster Home for tea and biscuits on few occasions. I understand now they should have protected the children, they didn't! My first day after being dropped off by social workers the Auntie was smiling allot while we were introduced to her, but as soon as the officials had left her smile disappeared!

Ordered to stand against the hall wall, Aunty gave me the many rules on pain of punishment. The rules I kept for the next nearly eight years! I was told never to enter any other part of the house other than the Dining Room, which was to be our living room!

The Dining Room was a room which was bare accept for a small hatch in the wall where we would receive Breakfast Dinner and Tea. Two steel legged tables and steel legged chairs were the only furniture. The number of chairs changed according to how many foster children were housed at the time.

The downstairs of the house was made up of a long hall with a playroom at the far end. The Foster families lounge toilet and a back door leading to a large lawn garden were also along this hall. Stairs from the hall led up to 6 bedrooms a toilet and bathroom. 3 of the six rooms where for the use of foster children, two of the three where made up of 3 beds in each and one was a single. I was commanded never to leave the bedroom after being put to bed, no talking under any circumstance. I saw the other rooms only once in eight years! I was confined to the dining room in the day when not at school.

I learned to hate the Dining Room with its bare white walls cold Marley floor tiles. A large double net curtained window allowed us to see over the privet bushes to the street outside again. I was commanded never to leave my chair, not to open the Curtains to look out! With a threat of punishment should I disobey.

The foster family where a real family, they ate separately and had their own lounge and playroom for their boys. Needless to say we never saw the boys, and only saw Auntie at authorised times i.e. bedtime breakfast and Teatime.

I often thought how nice it would be to play in the Foster families Play Room where there where toys and soft cosy furniture. I glimpsed in once when noticing the Foster Family boys playing with a large racing toy car track, they were laughing and having fun, but no foster children were allowed to enter the room or talk to the boys.

I learned what the punishment was one day at age 10. I had heard A playing and went into the room to play with him, he shouted at me to "get out" I said "no" he physically attacked me, I fought back, he was older taller and heavier than me but I was able to give him a bleeding nose. The Auntie hearing the commotion and a calling for his mummy came running into the room, dragged me from the room by my hair throwing me against the wall, demanding that I stay face to the wall while she attended her son.

I knew I was in trouble, but didn't realise how much until the big brother and the Uncle came home…. I had been stood face to the wall in the hall all afternoon not allowed to move! I was very tired by 6pm when the older son and his dad came home. They were called into their family lounge by the Aunty and I was scared. First the Father came out followed by the older son younger son and their mother.

They approached me from behind. I was dragged backwards by the father and older son to the floor, the father and older son held me down and called over the younger son, they said "I was to get what I deserved" the father ordered the younger son to sit atop of me and begin beating my face and body. I couldn't move...I was beaten repeatedly whilst they each repeated... "you stay out of the room and never approach our son again" I was then dragged up off the floor by the Father and eldest Son and ordered again to stand face to the wall, this time the father had brought his German Shepherd inside and ordered it to guard me...he told me the Dog would bite me if I moved!

I was bruised scratched with a bleeding nose and terrified. The dog guarded me for several hours, I was too scared to move then ordered to bed at 9pm!

CHAPTER 7

Fear and More Fear

It took many years to imagine how a young boy could process the brutality inflicted by these so called "Foster Carers". Each day in the foster home I sat in silence filled with dread. I remained quiet trying not to be noticed by the Foster family who I must not disturb! I was ordered threatened not to speak of the home to anyone at school, to return straight back when school was out. The impact on me was only apparent in my adult years.

Each day I stood alone in the playground, not mixing with the other children made me a target to further cruelty of the other kids. More than once a teacher asked me if I would be more comfortable at break times helping out in the classroom cleaning...anything to protect the kid with a squint who didn't smile mix or speak!

Learning anything felt difficult for me, my mind felt empty I couldn't grasp or feel interest in what was being said, just a constant dread of returning to the foster home! Each day I would race back to the home knowing I would be punished if not on time, returning to that room was my greatest fear I hated it. Waiting on my assigned chair in the dining room...being quiet not allowed to speak...waiting for food to be passed through the hatch.

Sometimes the other foster kids spoke in whispers which would immediately stop if Aunty was heard to be approaching. The foster kids black white large and small all sat quietly on their assigned seats...like me... we occasionally whispered to each other or just sat looking through white netted curtains to the street outside watching children passing playing. Each day I waited for mum or dad to take me home waiting watching and hoping, they never came!

Other fostered children often left and I never saw them again. I waited for many years thinking Mum or Dad would come for me... Christmas especially and birthdays, but they never did. I waited silently for nearly eight years ...I sat until my silence became me, no thoughts no words no sense of belonging. I stopped speaking and stopped feeling...an empty nobody! I tried for all those cold empty years not to be noticed wanting to disappear! The kids at school called me names...I would explode into instant rage punch kick scream and scratch until either I was beaten, or the other kid was. I would come away exhausted even as the victor! Each day at school I tried to make myself small.

My life felt empty, lonely and nothing! My isolation from other kids was made worse by my short pants squint and silence! At a "Special School" for slow learners at age 14yrs old I had to fight off the bullies daily sometimes being beaten by them. I did notice the bullying got less as I retaliated and they learned not to mess with the boy in short pants squinty eye and who never spoke! By 14yrs I hadn't learned much at all! I couldn't focus and ignored all learning and was sent to a Special School for slow learners! There I learned how to protect myself! This learning was to shield me for many years afterwards, it prepared me for the years and institutions to come.

I decided to run away from the Foster home at age 15. Life was about to get much harder and the Liverpool streets would become my new home.... I didn't know where I was going to go, but going I was! Food was served as usual in silence that day via the hole in the wall but I knew it was the last time! Curiously I felt something! Feeling anything was something new. I felt excited and scared at the same time feeling excitement was alien to me! This feeling made me feel alive! I had a plan and no plan, didn't have a clue where I was going. I was going to escape from this Foster Home where I had been placed for my own protection! It would be a joke if it wasn't such a tragedy....

My first attempt at running away from a children's home ended with my mother phoning the Social services to take me back to the home. It was this that taught me the true meaning and effects of being rejected of being unloved! Somewhere inside of me a child was screaming to be loved to be wanted and comforted and it affected me for many years afterwards! I had a vague memory of my Grandmother living somewhere in Liverpool city centre...that is where I was going to go! Grandmother would welcome me?

The next day after a night of tossing and turning in my bed I decided "I was going" ... The boy with the short pants squinty eye and no smile got a green public Bus which said City Centre. I knew I would eventually be missed and reported as missing so I had to keep my head down. Unfortunately, this was not easy as I had got on the Bus with no money! I lied to the ticket collector, that I had lost my fair he hummed and erred, but let me stay on the bus to the Centre... yes I was on my way...but to where?? I got off the bus by TG Hughes's Department Store facing the Adelphi Hotel close to the Bullring.

Vague memories of a time in this City came back to me; I vaguely knew this grandma "ninny Smith" from another time. She lived inside the Bullring a circular building of tenement blocks three storeys high, there was one entrance in and one exit out and was a scary place to be at night.

When I arrived it was evening, gangs of kids were hanging about the entrances and exits, they challenged and made threats towards me asking "hey short arse, what ye doin here, if ye don't live here, fuck off or we will beat the shit out ye" in rough thick nasal scouse accents. I was scared but was not going to back down, they must have sensed it and left me alone! I walked in the direction I remembered......I had to knock on a few doors but was rewarded when the door opened by my grandmother (ninny) who gave me my mums address and a couple of shillings to get the bus!

Arriving at a small upstairs flat next to a large green grassed park I knocked, a small stringy hard faced woman with dyed Auburn hair bright red lipstick and small beady eyes opened the door. She was my mum and she didn't recognise me! But I recognised her.

I felt nothing and said nothing for what seemed a long time, then recognition dawned and she exclaimed "It's you. How are ye son"? I wasn't sure how to answer she didn't approach me or give me a hug, not even "I missed you" so I just said "yes it's me" the door was held ajar for me to enter. I could smell hairspray cigarettes and cooking smells as I entered through the peeling green door into a poorly lit drab living room. It was a small flat two bedrooms' bathroom/toilet and lounge, a black cast iron hearth built into the wall and a very small kitchen with a Gas Cooker and sink.

The place was poorly lit, the furniture sparse and old, which consisted of a ragged faded Settee and a battered Armchair. An oval wooden framed black and white photograph, of a lady was hanging above the black cast iron hearth were a kettle was boiling. Standing in the kitchen and coming out to see who had entered was my sister Margaret older than me by one year. Margaret had never stayed in care for long as mum seemed to have favoured her over the years, while the rest of us remained in various Care Institutions. Margaret had red hair slim and looked like mom only younger "What ye doing here, have ye run away?" the Liverpool accent was very apparent. I replied "yes did a runner today" mom was standing to the side of the fire the back of her legs had a corn beef rash where she had spent too much time with her back to the fire. She was back combing her hair and spraying it, she told me there was no room for me and I would have to go back and anyway she was going out soon!

Not long afterwards there was a knock on the door. I knew it was the return journey back to the home! I remained quiet not knowing what to say, didn't have anything to say! I couldn't express my feelings and allowed myself to go in silence to the awaiting car. This was to become a repeated pattern in my life of allowing whatever came as an accepted natural course of events no questions asked!

I had begun to believe that this was the way life was and went round and round like this for the next 5 years! I had no idea until later that it was in my power to change my life in any way I desired but I had to find this out for myself and gain the desire!

I was on my way back to the Foster Home Dining Room a cold loveless place I thought I had escaped from! My mind just switched off....... It took many years of self-searching to find my memories and my mind again. Remembering brought pain anger depression denial blame acceptance and sadness, and freed me from the dark places of my mind where a child had hidden his pain!

CHAPTER 8

Slow Learner

In the foster home I was told by the foster parents that I never smiled or laughed! Could they really not see what they were doing to the children in their lack of care home! Did they not know how hurt and rejected we felt? The Foster carers had an opportunity to help the children feel loved worthwhile and valued, instead they did the opposite! I cowered alone in play grounds glued to fences.

I was forever waiting for Mum or Dad to come and get me. I refused to participate in the classroom. I was sullen withdrawn and a target for the other kids. I learned and discovered that bullies left you alone if you gave them a quick response! By and by they did get a quick response and left me alone. I found remembering lessons impossible nothing could gain or keep my attention because it was now me who didn't care!

Having a squint in my right eye until aged 14yrs earned me the school playground name of "Squinty Eye" that name really hurt me at school and fighting with name callers became almost a daily event. I was eventually put into a Learning Difficulties School because I wasn't responding in classes, wouldn't communicate with anybody not the teachers or other kids, nobody!

Having been identified in Junior School as a child who didn't appear to be responding with no interest in learning. I was sent to a Child Psychiatrist who gave me a test with some ink blots confirming

River Blue

I was a slow learner!? And then gave authorisation to send me to a Special School which appeared to be full of children just like me, sultry angry disinterested and difficult to manage. I learned nothing but low self-esteem, self-defence and the label of "slow learner" leading me falsely believe for many years I had no ability to learn!

Wow Psychiatry has something to answer for! I have thought about that Psychiatrist on occasions, it leaves me appalled! The missed opportunities they had to help me. I needed to be understood helped and rescued!

I went unnoticed labelled and further punished, not knowing why I felt so alone. I was isolating myself hurting and afraid. I had built unknowingly impenetrable psychological walls to protect myself. I had been rejected and it hurt me. I had become an empty shell, these feelings remained with me until I realised through awareness and self-study that I was damaged and needed repair! Later with medical training knowledge and experience I knew I was suffering P.T.S.S "Post-Traumatic Stress Syndrome" this knowledge led me to believe rightfully that I could conquer these acquired thoughts and emotions, that the condition was reversible but would take time.

I made it my mission to overcome my thoughts and feelings of self-depreciation. I read many Self-Help books and researched Counselling. I Studied and passed 5 O levels and an A Level in six months of Evening College. Trained successfully as a Registered Nurse. Gained several Dip Ed in Cognitive Behavioural Therapy and Counselling. Got a Cert Ed in Advice and Guidance. Trained as a Teacher built a Business and successfully learned Meditation and Reiki Healing Techniques in the mountains of India...I began to find true peace and self-healing

CHAPTER 9

Nightmares

As an adult I was able revisit my inner child and we faced together the powerful emotions of anger loneliness rejection sadness fear darkness. The terrifying emotions of my inner child flooded back to me and the awakened memories resurfaced. I remembered where one of my reoccurring nightmares had come from....as a child aged 9 years at school I had been locked in a pitch black abandoned air raid shelter on the back of the school field by a group of young boys who thought it would be fun! It was pitch black in the shelter; I had descended the stairs before the door slammed shut above.

I was terrified in the darkness with the smell of filth damp and dead creatures, sticky cobwebs and suffocating darkness. I could not find my way back to the stairs in the inky blackness. I groped about for about an hour in the dark blind bumping into walls discarded smelly rotting furniture. Each time my body touched anything my imagination cried out in terror thinking, dead bodies' rats' ghosts creepy crawlies and all manner of horrible imaginings! The products of a 9-year-old mind who was thinking he was trapped forever never to return to the world of light. Once remembered the nightmare ended never to return like magic, but it took thirty years to discover its origin. The problem was not only did I remember that incident but many memories came flooding back! I had Self-Imposed Selective Amnesia. I had unconsciously hidden away all that was too painful for my young mind to deal with, burying all traces of the pain deeply in my subconscious. The subconscious mind influences every aspect of an individual's daily life. Any help to gain conscious awareness of these buried memories and emotions brings healing and balance. Empowering that individual to gain a life worth living!

How could a child deal with rejection violence beatings and social psychological deprivation inflicted, by adults who deliberately used cruelty to feed the worms inside themselves and crush the lives of innocent children and adults in their care? I learned much later that several children placed into the hands of those deprived adults in the Liverpool Foster Care Home sadly and tragically committed suicide!...

CHAPTER 10

Escape to The Streets

The car and social workers who picked me up from mums took me to an overnight stay Children's Care Home a large Victorian building in Wootton. I was put straight to bed in a single room where I welcomed sleep...empty and sick. The next morning, I was taken back to the foster home. All the way there I knew I wasn't staying! Dreading the return even for a short while.

On my arrival back at the Foster Home, it was early morning. I was met with the false smile I had learned to know, a smile put on by Auntie when visitors were about...but I knew that as soon as they left all would return to the cold white room and isolation. Auntie was "disgusted" she said after social services had left, and if I didn't want to stay I "was welcome to leave" as "she didn't want me there" I stayed silent as a response from me would only invited punishment of further deprivation.

I was told not to leave the dining room all day, no food was given until six hours later when several of the other foster children returned from School! The food was always the same after a weekend. The Foster family had roast chicken with all the trimmings followed by pudding, we got the left over's in the shape of chicken pearl barley soup for several days afterwards. I hated the soup and envied the Foster family...the smells of their cooking filled the house but we always knew it wasn't for us.

Aunty after giving us our food through the hole in the wall retired to her lounge with a warm coal fire, television and carpet, a very cosy room nicely decorated, which we would be invited to sit in only when Social Services came to visit. Then we would find ourselves sitting smartly dressed in that room for as long as it took for Social Services to leave!

The Foster parents had it down to a fine art and Social Services enjoyed their cup of tea twice a year, the only question they ever asked me was "are you being good"? No wonder so many children in the sixties and seventies were so abused, the system was a cash cow for them all! They lived comfortably, while the Children's lives were devastated!

Several more months went by before I decided once more to leave. I can't remember where or how I got to know that mom had got a place outside of town. It was now very obvious to me that I was not wanted so this time I would just go and hope for the best! I was determined I would not return to mum again, but I didn't know where to run to!?

Escape I did and the streets of Liverpool became my home in between other institutional stays. I was 16 and life felt an empty miserable place for me. It is true what they say "misery loves company" and I found living from sofa to sofa sleeping in sheds to office buildings and cars. It wasn't much but it was all I had. I learned quickly how to survive. The other young boys I met had similar backgrounds to mine and I felt part of something and nothing. We drank wine and beer smoked cigarettes and pot and spent each day dodging the law and Social Services who were looking for me to return me back to institutional care...as legally I was still "A Ward of the Court" for my care and protection!?

I was caught again the day I took my sisters girlfriend to the pictures then back to mom's place who was never in so occasionally I could sneak in. I had been introduced to a girlfriend of my sister and went to the movies liking each other a lot we kissed and fondled each other in-between pretending to watch the movie. After the movie

Diamond in the Stone

was over we went back to my mom's place to continue our fumbling trying to have sex without success! Neither of us had any experience of sex so other than the fumble no intercourse took place. A look over my shoulder froze me, a Social Services person and policeman had entered the house, we hadn't shut the front door! We were both taken to the police station where I declined to say anything! Her parents took her home and I was charged with attempting to have sex with a person under age of consent, (she was the same age as me I believe!) While in police custody I was asked to put my name to several TIC's, "taken into consideration" these being unsolved vehicle crimes! They said if I agreed I would avoid going back to the home I dumbly signed.... then found myself put into a Juvenile Remand Centre to await the magistrates court decision which came after a month or two...

I was sentenced to a Probation Hostel in London! For 12mts the court told me but I again knew I was not staying and would abscond first chance! I had to stay in a remand home in London awhile which was actually a prison with bars on the widows and razor wired fencing! Tough guards in suits and some of the nastiest young men from all over the UK. Most of their stories where similar to mine....no parents, parental abuse, foster care, substance abuse, some of the inmates thought violence could get them anything. It was a school of hard knocks.

The victims were the weak who didn't stand up for themselves, because they were scared and why shouldn't they be? When they didn't fight back the victim ended up as they say in the Movies "someone's bitch" this meant they would be used abused in every conceivable way e.g. any property they may have had would be taken. The homosexual bully boys raped and buggered their victims making the life of a timid person a complete misery. I had learned the lesson at school never to be a victim; I did this by sending out the message very quickly not to mess with me.

There were several known bullies in the remand centre and I knew if I could whack at least one of them before they whacked me they would leave me alone. One evening the bully boys had commandeered the pool table, loud and thuggish like they didn't care! They believed they could push shove anyone then protect each other. They came to the end of their game and it was my turn to play. One bully boy told me to go and "f--- myself and get lost" this was the moment I was waiting for and they never saw it coming! The snooker cue I was carrying was just the job, I swung it hard and quick at the speaker who fell screaming to the ground his face covered with his hands, his bully mates came towards me. I swung and hit another then stood staring them in the eyes daring the next one to try, they backed off as they realised I was no push over!

    I played my pool game but all the time watching from the corner of my eye for potential repercussions from the bully boys….it never came and they left me alone from then on. I made no friends and kept myself aloof from the cliques of hard cases. Life at the remand home became routine until I was told I was being shipped out to London to the Probation Hostel. I wasn't worried as it meant I didn't have to return to "the home" ever again which suited me fine. I didn't know that home would haunt and affect me for so many years to come, I was damaged and nobody cared. Nobody showed me care in those years. The system wanted to sweep the rubbish as they saw it off the streets but in doing so the government had created breeding grounds of hate, violence, abuse and the next generation of prisoners! The institutions were thriving producing hardened criminals from damaged children. The drive to London seemed to take forever.

CHAPTER 11

Probation Hostel

I was told we were headed to a hostel in Lewisham which meant nothing to me. I did think it was going to be better than the streets of Liverpool. I was anxious and excited wondering what a hostel might be like. We arrived early afternoon in October it was cold raining.

The hostel appeared grim, grey and foreboding, the building was in a street lined with old Victorian houses. I was taken by my probation officer driver to the front door which was newly painted a glossy deep blue with a gleaming brass knocker in the shape of a lion's head. The door was answered by a small podgy 30 something male wearing baggy corduroy trousers and chunky grey woollen jumper, he beamed a great smile at me and my escort, bid us both welcome and asked us to follow him to the office based in the cellar.

We followed the house was quiet and spotlessly clean, we passed a huge brown oak staircase as we approached the cellar door beneath the stairs. When we got to the basement it was kitted out as an office, the desk was untidy, books appeared scattered here there and all over "right sit down you both and I will make a nice cup of tea" I was feeling wary, I had this smiley reception experience before and fully expected that as soon as my escort left, the real world would begin! We sat as tea was served with a couple of biscuits. This was starting to feel a bit weird! I never had someone be so nice to me what was the catch? "My name is Trevor I am supervisor here my job is to help you settle in" I felt suspicious why was he being so nice, was it an act? he went on..." here you will be expected to work and earn your keep, we will find you a job and you will earn a wage" it all felt surreal.

I kept thinking "what's the catch" he said "lets show you around and then give you some time to yourself before the lads get home from work" we said goodbye to my escort at the door. Trevor showed me upstairs and stated "this is your room; you will be sharing with two others who I will introduce you to later when they get home. But just have a wonder about in the meantime get used to the place and find your way about".

This was amazing he was still smiling and being nice! I was starting to feel I would be ok if the cheerful niceness was real...... sadly it wasn't and I don't mean Trevor. He continued his pleasant helpful self for all the time I knew him, no, my real world began when the others started to arrive from work.

The two I was sharing with, looked me up and down, asking what you in for? I wasn't sure what they meant by "in for" and my lack of understanding appeared to irritate them. I knew I couldn't allow them to think I was weak but so far they hadn't said anything abusive. Paul and Tony stood just staring at me looking me up and down. Tony was the short dark haired stocky one with a mean look about him, he had a Newcastle accent and looked like he may be able to handle himself in a fight. Paul was curly and blond with an Elvis slicked back haircut, he was taller than me and Paul chewing gum stated "you're a bloody nonce" now I knew things where about to get serious. I had learned in the remand centre and on the streets that a "nonce" was somebody who played with children! If you were called it you better be ready to beat the crap out of someone, there was no greater insult than this.

My heart began to pump, I knew it was a challenge, my mind was working out the best likely way to catch them off guard and do some damage to one or both. They were two strides in front of me this would make surprise hard as they'd see it coming. I needed to get closer and Liverpool blag came to my recue, I looked both in the eyes as I stated, "I don't know what you think I am and don't give a f---" I had taken two steps forward to the left of Tony knowing I could whack him before Paul could see it, but just then Trevor entered the room saying "I see you've met your new roommate, tea is ready down stairs so come on otherwise there will be nothing left the other lads will scoff the lot" he stood to one side to allow us all to pass to the stairs, both lads looked straight at me, snarled something turned toward the door and went down the stairs. Trevor looked at me and asked "everything alright"? "Yes we were just getting to know each other" I said heading past him to make my way down stairs...I knew this wasn't over!

It was unfinished business and knew I had to make my mark and rapid, to avoid any other crap that would go down if I didn't turn it around quick. The dining room was large with dark polished wooden floor boards, two long oak tables with a bench running each side Trevor said "that's your seat, no 3" I approached my seat Tony and Paul slid along the wooden bench towards each other to block me from sitting down....it was now or never "excuse me lads you're in my seat move"! Both looked up at me mouthed "f-- off nonce" Tony was nearest, I grabbed the back of his head and smashed it down as hard as I could into his soup bowl.

He had no chance to recover before I hit him with my fist to the back of his head he was dazed but Paul was up and lashed a fist straight into my mouth. I toppled backwards holding on to Paul's shirt, both of us mouthing obscenities at each other. We rolled on the floor trying to get a position where we could strike the other.

I felt myself lifted by my hair bodily off the oak floorboards and away from Paul, I was pulled backwards my arm was twisted behind my back. I was held by Trevor another Supervisor several feet away held Paul. Both of us struggling to get at each other but it was no use against the strength and well trained lever hold of our Supervisors. We were frog marched out of the dining room down stairs to the office, here they let go of us. We were each at opposite corners of the office. "Right you two" said Trevor "what's going on? We will not tolerate this behaviour, so speak" neither Paul or I spoke, we knew we were in trouble, we both knew also that you don't speak "to the man" the unwritten street law! "I am only ever going to let this behaviour go once, the next time I will report it, which means you will both be re sentenced for breaking your probation order, do you understand me?" we both said "yes" Paul was asked to return to the hall, I was to stay.

After Paul had left I was asked to sit down on a chair facing the desk. Trevor said "We are disappointed this is usually a peaceful place and our lads go on to better themselves in life after spending time here, so what's going on?" I stared vacantly not knowing how to respond, his voice was kind and he seemed genuinely concerned.

I was not used to being considered in any way, I felt awkward, I felt he was genuinely interested. I told him what I had been called, that I had to protect myself from attacks, settle it or become a victim.

He was reading my file and said, "I can see your point of view, but fighting is not the way to settle it" he suggested, he would gather the lads together and explain the situation to them, he was referring to the charge of my bungling attempt to have sex. The meeting with the other lads took place where I gave my side of the story, explaining that at the time it happened I had refused to speak when asked by police. This resulted in the parents of the girl allowing the police to press charges even though we were both under the age of consent. I had no Parents interested! And being male I was considered the offender!

Trevor read the report on this charge to the lads and re assured them. I asked how they had got the information Paul said "he read it on my file" Trevor "well now and again we have been known to leave the office unlocked" Paul or Tony had seen my file and assumed that the charge meant I was a "nonce". We went back up to the dining room where he outlined to 8 young men, the circumstances of my actions resulting in the charge and my probation order. The hall was silent and I felt self-conscious, but didn't let these feelings show. "Right you lot break it up and get on with your evening, and no more trouble from anyone....is that understood"? The evening consisted of recreation time, we could play table tennis pool or any number of games, or just hang out and chat in the large games room. Paul and Tony eyed me for a while but didn't approach, later in our bedroom we chatted, sleep was a welcome friend as I drifted off that night. The morning started at 7am, we each dressed washed. In the dining room nobody tried to stop me from sitting down breakfast was a noisy but peaceful affair. The other lads went off to their jobs in and around London.

I was asked to be ready to visit a prospective employer who may consider giving me a job in a steel furniture factory as a labourer the interview was short. I was told what was expected of me, start and finishing times and wages. I would be expected to pay board and lodgings for the Hostel, the little left over, I could spend or save...wow it sounded great. The factory work was manual work, sweeping and getting breakfast and lunch orders from local cafe for the workers. I liked the job and got on reasonably with all. Life for several months at the Hostel was uneventful, I was taught to wash iron and mend my own clothes, tidy my room and do weekend chores. After 3mts a dozen or so workers were laid off at the factory, including me. I was found a job in a large Dry cleaning factory, it was a job easy to do and I settled and liked it. I met a girl my own age and dated for several months, we would go the pictures and hang out around the town on my days off. One day while having a break, I tried to drive the works van, big mistake! I had never driven and drove it into the factory wall causing damage to the bumper.

I was so scared I was going to end up in trouble so decided to run away. There was another hostel boy working with me and we agreed to abscond together. The day came when we would be going to get sandwiches for the workers, we would then have a little money to spend on getting to London City, it seemed like the place to start. Wrong! It was awful! London is a terrible place to be homeless without money and on the run. We were hungry most of the time but after 2 months we knew the warmest places to sleep at night. In the day we wandered aimlessly in and out of shops, we even went to the Houses of parliament were we got escorted out by the Concierge as scruffy intruders!

CHAPTER 12

Streets of London

The boy I had absconded with was very good at sneak thieving i.e. going into offices and staff rooms of hospitals and anywhere coats and bags could be rifled. We managed not to starve on what he was able to steal…I didn't have the courage to do it but he was fearless. We met other homeless, some very sorry sights messed up on drugs or alcohol. Unwashed ragged people aimlessly wandering and surviving the streets of London. Sleeping at night was always a problem, first you had to find a warm dry safe place.

My favourite place to sleep was the baggage compartments at the railway stations, but we would be thrown out by security police each morning at 5.30 am! The 5.30am wake up was always the most miserable especially when it was cold wet and we were hungry. Another place we would sleep in, was workmen's sheds on building sites, were there would be Workmen donkey jackets and tarpaulin to cover us, it would be reasonably warm and safe as long as we got out before 8am each morning.

Homosexuality was very much in the closet and unlawful in the 60's, and we being young lads were constantly pursued by the odd desperate gay guy. One night we had been spotted going into Euston Rail Station to sleep in luggage compartments but were moved on by security when entering. We decided to sleep on the park in front of Euston Station. It was damp and cold on the grass. Suddenly I was

Diamond in the Stone

woken by movement behind me! I was shocked to find on turning some guy cuddling up to me! I was up and running in a second with my mate behind me, it scared the daylights out of us both...This same man kept turning up time after time following us everywhere for days! He was smartly dressed, but to us he looked like a weirdo.

I remember being scared that he might kill and rape us, my run away mate suggested we pretend to make friends with this man, let him take us to his home, beat him up and rob him omg! No way I thought he may kill us. I went to the Railway security police the next day when he showed up again! I pointed him out and the security men gave chase, from then on we never saw him again. London felt scary after so we hitched a lift to Brighton.

It was bitterly cold on the coast, the wind and rain made me feel miserable and depressed. The fairground was the warmest safest place we could find were we slept in the cave exhibits of paper Mache cavemen which were lit at night and we were sheltered from the wind and rain. Food was plentiful from the waste bins around the Park Cafes Restaurants and Supermarkets. We were spotted one night going into the Fairground so couldn't go back there, we then slept under the privet bushes surrounding the fairground until one night about 1am in the morning, a hand came through the bushes just above were we were sleeping, we both watched it terrified, holding our breaths as the hand appeared to be searching about in the bush, then we saw it grasp a small parcel and disappear.

I was so scared at the time. I never breathed until the hand disappeared afterwards I had a panic attack! I couldn't stop my breathing which was rapid and totally out of control. I said to my mate "we have to get out of here" so we headed back to the motorway north going in the direction of Liverpool and Manchester. Hitching a lift with a friendly truck driver we got as far as Warrington.

The driver took us as close as he could on route and said goodbye 2 am in the morning leaving us at a layby on the outskirts of Warrington. It was cold, dark and wet, we were freezing and tired. Where we had been dropped we could make out the occasional house

River Blue

and what appeared to be a farm in the distance. Maybe we could find shelter until morning. After a long cold walk we followed a farm path as quietly as we could, if we were caught we would be taken back to the hostel. The darkness made it difficult to find anything like a barn, but we kept searching in the darkness. An automatic light went on at the front of the house as we crept by illuminating all around us! We ran in the direction of the road hearing voices but couldn't make out the words. On reaching the exit gate of the property we half ran on the damp grass of the roadside stumbling in muddy puddles... miserable wet cold and tired we walked not knowing where we were going in the darkness.

After forever I heard a car its headlights getting closer we jumped into the bushes to hide. We had learned to be suspicious of night time cars! And passing police could take us back. We stayed in the bushes until the car passed then trudged on. The flashing blue lights came minutes after, we ran but we were lifted bodily off the ground by two uniformed policemen "right you pair in you get, you can tell us what you have been up to at the station" it was warm in the car and I was relieved to be out of the cold.

We must have looked a right sight with dirty clothes and faces muddy trainers, dirty soggy hostel anoraks, hair soaking wet. At the police station we were put in separate cells which smelt of stale urine cigarette smoke and damp blankets. Graffiti scrawled pictures and writing scratched on every surface. The banging heavy steel doors echoed inside and out making me jump each time one slammed shut. I could hear drunken slurred raised voices swearing shouting from somewhere outside my cell. A small window was set high up on the back wall, a wooden board attached to the far wall there was a folded grey blanket. The window frame was all steel with small panes of solid glass. I pulling the blanket around me its heavy and coarse weight began to warm my freezing wet body. I sat and waited...the steel door echoed once again as a tall grey haired policeman stepped in to the cell and held out a steaming hot cup of tea. I took it gratefully, and the door slammed once again making me jump.

The tea was hot, milky and sweet, I was warming up and tiredness soon overtook me and I slept fitfully, the swearing, hollow sounding voices and slamming steel doors filtering into my mind making a sound sleep impossible. The cell was as empty as me, I was accepting of what ever came next, no questions asked. I was woken around 7am by a voice calling me to "get up, the sergeant wants a word" I stumbled from my wooden board, still dazed and sleepy.

The door security lock made a cracking sound as the key was turned, and swung open. A shorter policeman, entered the cell and questioned me relentlessly, "who was I", "where was I from"? "What was I doing"? "Did I intend to burgle the house whose path we had wandered up"?? The questions went on and on, as he scribbled in his little black notebook. I didn't tell him I had absconded, said I had no intention of burgling, that I had thumbed a lift to Liverpool after running away from home. I thought I would be taken back to London, but we were both eventually charged with attempted burglary! The police knew it appeared that we were on the run and had broken our probation order to reside at the Hostel. This was another charge! And I was driven back to London the next morning to a Juvenile Remand Centre, where I waited nearly two months to attend court, it was very much as the first remand centre, filled to busting with testosterone bullying and constant challenges. I met each challenge, fighting at least once a week to ensure nobody would bother me it always worked, find the biggest, and punch them out, then mind your own business.

CHAPTER 13

Approved School

Eventually I was to be sentenced to a Youth Offenders Institution in Southport, Wirral. St Thomas Moors for attempted burglary and breaking my Probation order. A real school of hard knocks I was to find out quickly. I was seventeen, it was so crazy looking back, no matter what, I always ended up "locked away" I was growing accustomed to it. I learned what was expected of me with a sense of grudging obedience, biding my time to run once more!

The Approved school was a large mansion, very old mostly made of York stone dark oak panelling and red tiled floors. Dormitories, with up to 10 youth in each dorm, about 30 young damaged men placed there to learn the rules and discipline of society! A place where they could be hidden from the rest of the world.... each of us knew the ropes and each had similar backgrounds, rejected uncared for, parents with substance abuse issues, inadequate parents who had stumbled into parenthood without a clue of what to do next, single mothers surviving one broken relationship after another. They too been abused and some even battered by reluctant fathers who preferred to drink and be out and about. It was the norm in the back streets of Liverpool and the children paid the price. Institution after Institution and on and on it went. Here we all were fighting angry and sad, "the disposed of" you had to get tough and fight let no one in. Say "yes" to the man and kick the crap out of any one that messed with you. At least 80% of the youth I met knew the score by age 15 and 16 yrs. old. We gave grudging respect to those who knew the score, and pitied them that didn't!

I once again at this place made my statement very quickly. Being challenged first day gave me the opportunity I needed, and I made my mark! Nobody messed with me. I was respected because I fought any and every one who didn't show respect. Didn't always win the fights I had, but even so, they knew what to expect.

I was approached one day in the dorm by a spotty faced tall stout loudmouth, he demanded that I "give him my pocket money that week or else" I told him "f....k off". Then I waited for the time when he would approach me again. I knew that would happen soon. He was much bigger older and stronger than me so I watched him and he watched me! it was a waiting game and we both knew the score. Friday was pocket money day when each of us would be given a couple of pounds which we could use to buy toiletries sweets etc. As expected I was approached while walking down a corridor to my assigned living room, a room where you could watch the TV or just sit and read. The bully followed me several steps behind with a smirk arrogant look on his face.

It had to be somewhere we would not be seen by the housemen, the male guardians in their suits and ties who would if they caught us fighting withdraw privileges such as weekend visits to town pocket money or TV, or if serious be taken back to court for another sentence. I was careful and waited in the living room and as expected bully boy came in, "giz yer money divvy" he demanded in a thick menacing scouse accent, "come and get it dick head" I replied, he rushed at me, but I was ready and swung fast and hard connecting with his jaw and he fell to the ground and I stood over him awaiting a response, he muttered some profanity but stayed down and I walked away feeling proud!

I had showed him and I wouldn't be hearing from him again in a hurry. I would always be watching and waiting for the return match… it didn't happen, he left me alone. It was a tough place alright but there where good days too. Like when we headed to the fair in Southport Town Centre and hung out at the local coffee bars. It was 1969 and Skinheads were the hard case gang members who made themselves look tough. The uniform was faded jeans, turned up above the ankles, Dr Martin army boots and Ben Sherman tartan Shirts with buttoned down collars. Hair shaven to the skull and a swagger that threatened all in our path. I became a skin head, thinking I looked smart and tough; we hung out at every opportunity at the sea side coffee bars, spat on the ground acting loud and aggressive. I felt I had respect, we were just scared children really! But we felt powerful and protected in our gang. Our mission was to fight the mods and the bikers. Never did fight any! The mods stayed away and the bikers were mature adults tough as old boots!

I was dared one day by my Skinhead pals to go into a Hells Angels Pub.....I couldn't lose face in front of the lads and went in! Lots of shiny Motor Bikes were parked outside. I swaggered in as bold as brass looking around giving them my most threatening look! The men with long hair beards and smelly jeans looked me up and down bemused by my presence… I heard the words "piss off you little fart" fear told me to leave which I did very quickly! I had scored with my skinhead pals who now thought I was rock hard! Little did they know that I had nearly peed my wrangler jeans… I was terrified!

CHAPTER 14

Detention Centre

My time at the Approved School came to an end when after 12 months I'd had enough. I wanted to see my brothers and sisters so unscrewed a window and shimmied down the drain pipe in the night and headed to Liverpool. I had stayed nearly twelve months; I was now 17yrs old. I got to Liverpool after travelling all night, several lifts from lorry drivers got me to where I knew several of my family now lived. I fully expected mom would send me back again but went there feeling resentful that she didn't care about me.

That night I drank a bottle of QC wine and was so drunk I told my mom what I thought of her and she called the police. I staggered out into the street where I was to meet and get to know the street lads who hung about all day and dodged the law all night. We got drunk, stoned and slept from sofa to sofa where ever we could get in for the night. So began my second initiation into the streets of Liverpool. One of the lads pulled up in a car one night and several of us got in, he drove like a lunatic, with no road skills whatsoever, we laughed and jeered him on from the back seat until a Police car gave chase. Our driver went over islands skidded and screeched up and down lanes and roads of the housing estate… next thing I knew, he had stopped the car and everyone but me got away! I was taken into custody. When it was found I had absconded from Approved School I was charged with breaking my court order and taking and driving away? Driving with no licence or insurance? I couldn't drive! I wasn't driving! But I got charged anyway. I was sentenced to Detention Centre; known as the "Short Sharp Shock"

    I found out why from day one! It was hard-core. You were in army huts with 20 other youths of varying ages. We were given disciplined Army training every day for three months. Up at 6.00am, drilled and marched in boots for the first hour boots had to shine! Then into the gymnasium for one hour before breakfast! The gym was used for "circuit training" that was an hour's set routine and repetition of bench presses, sit ups, weight lifting, running, press ups and general torture! I saw many collapse from sheer exhaustion vomiting and losing consciousness. It hurt like hell but a refusal attracted a stay in the Isolation block and further drilling on the yard.

    The Prison Officers were tough pan faced no nonsense disciplinarians we called each "Sir". When it came to the daily routine a refusal or aggression was met with swift disciplined restraint. These men where tougher than us we knew it and respected them or suffered the consequences. After breakfast we stood to attention silently on the yard for inspection of boots and dress code then marched army style to the concrete shop. Here we mixed concrete for eight hours a day putting the concrete mix into vibrating moulds for paving slabs sold to government institutions throughout the UK.

    Talk about being fit! We were all as fit as any serving soldier and more so. Evenings we had 2 hours of respite when we were allowed to play board games in the recreation room. Each day "Sir" woke us up with shouting and pulling off our blankets. We marched to the long white tiled shower room and toilets and had exactly 20 minutes to be washed showered and dressed in full army kit. Before we could leave for morning routine every piece of our kit…vests trousers shirts bedding all had to line up neatly with the next bed! "Sir" would hold a string from one end of the dorm to the other, ensuring every boys bed and kit was perfectly aligned, if not the whole lot of us would have to do push ups while "Sir" wrecked every bed! We then had to start again neatly aligning everything we had until "Sir" was satisfied.

Diamond in the Stone

Whoever was found to be responsible attracted punishment from the other lads later in many cruel and violent ways. The classic was "razorblades in the soap of the offender" several times; I witnessed blood and the screams of the unfortunate victim. Others would be set about in the showers kicked punched beaten until they were left semi-conscious! Yes, it was definitely a "Short Sharp Shock" but it made me physically fit and hard as rocks! It wasn't a deterrent or rehabilitation just cruel and Punishing-I did learn to be tidy! Three months later I was being discharged standing stiff to attention in front of the Governor's desk a "Sir" on either side of me. I was given a lecture on the value of self-discipline and staying out of trouble. My eyes straight ahead responded with a loud "Yes Sir" I did an about face on the spot like a professional Soldier and was marched out the gate strong cocky and very fit.

I felt on top of the world breathing in the free air. I had been given a free train Ticket and small amount of pocket money. I had nowhere to go, but headed to Liverpool once again. Looking back, I don't know how without a home without a job without money without support what they the Authorities expected the outcome to be! It was inevitable I now see; I was going nowhere! Arriving back in the old neighbourhood I didn't have a clue where to go.

I found several old street mates who welcomed me home and enjoyed some of the stories of my "Short Sharp Shock" Detention centre had given me Street Cred and I enjoyed the respect the guys gave me. Again staying from Sofa to Sofa, joy riding, getting drunk or stoned, shoplifting food and other necessary items in the day. Partying wherever as I settled back in. Marijuana weed, rocky pot was common in the streets and the nights passed away in a stoned relaxed stupor; this led me to become a Dealer and make some cash. It was easy to buy cut it and sell to who ever wanted it. I smoked my profits and partied with "fair-weather friends". I loved listening to music Pink Floyd and Moody Blues being my favourite bands. But all this partying ended when I took another ride in a stolen car and stupidly agreed to accept a TIC, (taken into consideration charge) of Burglary.

River Blue

I was this time remanded into Risley Remand Prison. This was a notoriously harsh place where many had taken their own lives while awaiting sentencing. I had reached the big league, home of the more mature criminally minded violent offenders, and the victims of this particular corrupted unjust penal system. It was a proper prison Razor Wire Guards and bars. 2 sometimes 3 to a cell. Bunk beds in a small cramped space stinking of sweaty feet filthy bodies and unemptied "Plastic Piss Pots" Faeces and stale Urine fermented each day stinking until prisoners were allowed to empty them out at "Slop Out" three times a day. Slop out was the time when scores where settled and deals were made by prisoners.

Fights and stabbings were the norm, you had to watch your back and stand up for yourself. You could end up beaten by the Guards or Prisoners, raped tortured and bullied and many suicides occurred as a result! It was 700 prisoners ruled over by some sadistic and violent Prison Officers. These corrupt officers took great pleasure in entering the cell of any who opposed them or broke the rules. They would beat the prisoner with truncheons fists, kick with shiny army booted feet and walk away laughing! Slamming the steel door behind them leaving the prisoner beaten and battered. Years later the cruelty and sadistic behaviour and suicides where investigated.

The corrupt Prison staff were brought to justice many years too late for the victims. But it is also fair to say the Officers where sometimes the victims as they would find themselves like one brutal Officer did, beaten and thrown over the landing crashing down on to the steel mesh several cell blocks down with loud cheering from the inmates!

CHAPTER 15

Borstal

My sentence after 5 months on remand at Risley was a year in "Borstal" A place I was told "where men would be sorted from the boys" where the systems juvenile failures came together under one roof" I had heard about it from others I met along the way, the stories I was told left me more than apprehensive and fearful, and I was also told it was hard to impossible to escape once there.

On getting to Borstal I discovered it was a longer version of the "Short Sharp Shock" The tough Officers were in civilian suits and ties. So for me other than the loss of freedom it held no great surprises. The inmates where bigger but so was I! Settling in there was allot easier than other places I had found myself. There were the usual thugs to contend with and contend I did, but I was now starting to think for myself. Institutions had become a regular event and I went with the flow, surviving had become a way of life, in fact surviving was my life!

On arrival I was given a Prison Number a blue striped Shirt and grey Trousers, prison issue Shoes and Boots Vests Underpants Socks and Bedding Toothbrush and Soap. I was shown to a double cell which I was to share with a Newcastle lad. We got on well, he didn't speak much and neither did I so it worked! John my cell mate over time told me his story and it was very much like mine. Abandoned at an early age he had taken to the streets and had spent many years

River Blue

in one institution after another for petty crimes. He too had become hardened and tough. He was quiet but the several times I saw him fight told me he had come here the hard way. He had taken some training in his youth as a boxer and he was fast and mean. We paired off and enjoyed relative peace from some of the other usual rubbish that went on.

We were both assigned to outside work detail and enjoyed the manual labour of digging and clearing up several acres of marshy grassland surrounding the Borstal. There were 7 other lads on the work detail accompanied by a tough seasoned Officer who didn't take any rubbish and expected us to just get on with it. We did get on with it Summer and Winter! I got to know a couple of the guards who turned out to be pretty good blokes all in all. You did as you were told and got on with whatever they gave you to do. Now and again you could find yourself in a fight but nothing to write home about.

We were fed well, kept fit and treated well on the whole. One Officer did attack me after I called him a name, he had me up the wall by my throat but let go when I explained through a closed off wind pipe that he was a f.....g bully with a stick. He was a big beggar broad and tall, maybe he was just having a bad day. He let go and put me on report. I stood in front of the Governor next morning; I lost my privileges for a week, and lost my outside work detail job. Being re assigned to the Electric Cable stripping shop were you spent eight hours daily stripping greasy tarred linings from old electrical cable.

It was dirty and monotonous work in a long cold wooden shed. One day I even contemplated cutting the end of my finger off so I could be taken to hospital and possibly escape. As it turned out I nearly lost my whole arm! When my hand got caught in the cable stripping machine omg I screamed so loud. I was terrified as my hand was dragged into the two revolving circular cutting blades. Luckily enough, the prisoner facing me managed to hit the emergency off switch. I went to hospital to fix my fingers which were squashed and gashed then did not have to work in The Electric Wire Stripping Shop anymore.

I eventually applied to work in the Kitchens and got the job. It was a step up and always warm, and I got the best food. I peeled vegetables scrubbed the kitchen floors made the bread and washed dishes. Giant electric steel vats of stew were always bubbling away and served to the lads at dinner and tea times, we were well fed. I liked working in the Kitchen had a couple of fall outs with other lads in the Kitchen but that was Borstal life and went with the territory. I worked hard kept my head down and nobody bothered me too much. I had become resigned to Institutional life, accustomed to whatever came next, it didn't scare me anymore! This registered I'm sure with those who otherwise would have given me grief, nobody did mess with me in or after Borstal. I was quiet sullen angry and ready to explode at any hint of threat. I had been rehabilitated from an innocent child to a criminalised hard streetwise youth with no prospects or future. I heard many say "I'm not coming back" when I was in Borstal but I met them later on in HMP Walton and Manchester HMP Strangways Prison!

CHAPTER 16

A Little Taste of Freedom

Leaving Borstal, I was again lost for somewhere to go and headed back to the Liverpool streets where I considered home! It was a dilemma each time I found myself free of where I should go? I knew only the streets and those that inhabited them who I naively considered my friends...I know now they were not! They like me where lost and I imagine as lonely as me.

How the hell I survived this crap is still a big mystery to me and I'm proud to have turned out ok! But material accumulation and ego are not and shouldn't be the measure of the character of a man. So I was in the streets again confused no plans no dreams no friends no family an empty shell. I got off the train and caught the bus. I had 20 pounds in my pocket with a letter to the DWP saying I had been released from Borstal which entitled me to claim "benefits"! I slept sofa to sofa meeting up with previous acquaintances drank got stoned and endured each day.

I was always glad to sleep as the world disappeared from view for a while but reality was always there in the morning. I always had a feeling of dread and emptiness, if I could sleep longer it would shorten the day. I smoked "pot" in the day and night to escape what had become my reality. I sold "pot" to get by. It was the emptiness the nothingness that sometimes threatened to smother me, where ever I went in the streets it was the same, like a hamster on a wheel I went round and round, starting nowhere ending nowhere.

Loneliness and anger were my constant companions I took them everywhere. I was lost but I didn't know it! I was now eighteen years old and still homeless this had become the norm. It didn't register in my mind that I could change it and I had no inclination to change it. I thought this was just the way it was so got on with it! I think it was George Harrison who wrote "if you don't know where you're going any road will take you there" I didn't know where I was going and didn't care, but where ever it was I was going there! It was a pointless depressing life devoid of any sense of joy.

I had heard from someone inside that in the Isle of Man you could find work in the Hotels as kitchen porters or waiters, so I decided to give it a shot. My younger Brother decided also to come with me. The crossing on the boat at night was horrendous with huge waves driving rain storms in inky blackness. Powerful winds made me feel the boat may sink and be lost in the sea! Cold Sick and tired we arrived after what seemed an eternity with nowhere to go! We visited every Hotel in Douglas, looking for work and luck was on our side. We were offered a job as live in as "kitchen Porters" at a large Hotel on the cliff side. The kitchen was enormous, our job was to wash the pots and pans and keep the kitchen tidy. The Chef was a Scottish no crap boss and made sure we worked hard.

We started at 6am and finished at 7:30pm. The room given to us to share was very small with 2 single beds a chair table clean and warm. Our meals didn't cost us anything and we often helped ourselves from the kitchens freezer at night to the best of everything available. My brother was a slim built good looking quiet man with bright red hair, had a great sense of humour and constantly made me laugh taking the mickey out of the other staff and guests when they were not in earshot. At night we went down to the promenade area where there were pubs and several night clubs.

Meeting up with others like us out for a good time. Lots of Scottish young men and girls made the evening's great fun, we laughed got drunk and partied at every chance I was actually living and enjoying this time! Our day back at the Hotel began as usual with a hangovers and trying to scrape ourselves off the beds with throbbing heads stumbling over each other, trying to wash and get down to the kitchen for 6am. The Chef always went crazy if anyone was late and would throw pots pans and anything else he could while swearing and shouting, and generally making an ass of himself.

We got to the kitchen that morning just before six am and immediately began to wash any dishes and pots used the night before. One of the other kitchen porters, a 20year old from Manchester built like a rugby player shouted at my brother and threw a pan into the sink causing it to splash all over the place sending soapy warm water all over me my brother and the floor. He thought this was hilarious and added insult to injury by calling my brother a "scouse twat" my brother went straight at him but he was too slow, and the porter head butted him, knocking him backwards to the ground then began kicking while swearing…I pulled the porter backwards slamming him into the racks of pots and pans, he was off balance and that was the end for him and I beat him.

It should have been the end of it, but the chef hearing the clatter and shouting demanded that the police be called…my brother and I scarpered at the sound of those words knowing it would result in a criminal charge. We raced to our room, quickly packed our bags and headed off to town only to be picked up by Police several hours later. We had already agreed that if we got picked up I was to take it saying "it was me who beat him" I felt obliged, my brother was younger and had not yet experienced prison and I didn't want him to. My brother was released and I was charged with assault.

CHAPTER 17

Prison

I was remanded in the Isle of Man Prison a small 40 prisoner affair which had great views over the sea, you could catch a tan lying under the cell prison bars and I did. I was sentenced to twelve months' prison. If I had served it in the Isle of Man it would have been a holiday, but I was transferred to HMP Walton after a month to serve my sentence.

Handcuffed to two burly plain clothes officers made it hard to enjoy the trip back. I couldn't even go the toilet without one or the other being with me. I felt like a hard-core criminal and was treated as such all the way there. People stared and made whispered comments, kids pointed it was so embarrassing. Arriving in England via Speke Airport, I was informed we would be picking up another Prisoner from Cheapside Police Station. Handcuffed I was driven to Liverpool City Centre.

I was ordered out of the car and we entered Cheapside Police Station in Liverpool. It looked a hundred years an old grey Victorian stone and concrete building. I was escorted handcuffed still to the Cells which where dark and drab Names and graffiti was scratched into the dirty grey walls. A wooden bench was hinged to a side wall, a grey blanket and dirty white plastic mug sat on the bench like they were expecting me. The heavy steel riveted door slammed behind me like thunder. I paced the cell reading the names of previous occupants

River Blue

scratched into the walls with dates and pictures scratched next to them. I was jolted back to reality by the door opening and a tall young man about 21 was shoved roughly into the cell.

He shouted some abuse at the Police Officer who ignored him slamming the Cell door shut. My Cell mate had short cropped blond hair and a scowl on his handsome angry face. He looked me up and down sizing me up, I stared back unflinching and asked him "what they got you for" he had been to court that day and had been sentenced to 3yrs in Prison and was on his way to HMP Walton. What he did next came as a bit of a shock "keep an eye out for the screws" he barked as he slid under the wooden bed attached to the wall. He began to pull and work loose the steel L bracket supporting the wooden bench! I stood transfixed and bemused not quite sure what the hell he was up to.

It became clear though when after half hour he had one hinge removed! The bracket he had worked loose was L shaped twelve inches both sides. "What are you going to do with that" I asked, "they are not getting me to Walton" he stated "so how you going to stop them" … "wait and see" he stated as he put the L shape down the back of his trousers! "They will spot that when they rub you down" …. "Not if you distract them when they begin to search me" … "you want me to help you escape, that will get me extra time if your sussed" I was really worried but thought I could create a distraction and if he got caught I would be in the clear. We chatted idly about nothing, he was worried and so was I, as we waited for the Officers to return and put us in the Meat Wagon (transport vehicle).

After an hour we heard footsteps coming our way along the hollow corridor outside the cell. My cell mate got up checking the fit of the steel down his back decided he would lay it so an arm of the L pointed outward, it was crazy! He looked like he definitely had something down his trousers from the back, the Officer would search him beginning from the front, so as long as the distraction took place just after front rub down he may just get away with it but I doubted it! The key turned in the steel cell door, a Police Officer swung it open "right you two by the door for rub down now" the other prisoner went first my heart was beating like a drum.

The Prisoners back to me and the Officer began his rubdown, around the collar down the arms open the mouth behind ears and then down the sides downwards to the outside of the legs then inside legs, this was my only chance to distract before he began the back search. I shouted "I'm not going" and stepped to the back of the Cell. The other Prisoner was pushed to one side, the Officer came menacingly toward me "oh yes you are son" grabbing me by the shoulder, the other prisoner winked back at me as I was frog marched roughly to the door to be searched.

We were handcuffed and escorted along the corridor to a steel back door which led to an enclosed yard. Several Officers on each side of us we were ordered into what looked like a Horse Box they called the "Meat Wagon" Any time now they would catch the other prisoner as he attempted to board with the steel hinge down his back" but they didn't! We climbed several narrow steel steps into the Meat Wagon. Inside was a secured driver's area and six double steel grated doors three each side with room for four prisoners in each. The other Prisoner and I were the only passengers on this trip to HMP Walton and told to enter the same cubicle! A miniature Cell with a short plank either side, walls reinforced with sheets of thin riveted steel. A small secured ventilation slit high up on the outside wall allowed some natural light through its frosted wire glass.

Our handcuffs were taken off and we sat down opposite each other, he had managed to get this far with the steel down his back! I now knew what he had in mind for this tool. As soon as the Cell door slammed shut he was feeling about the surfaces of riveted steel for weak points, where he could prise away the steel plate. He was going at it for an hour before it began to give, he pulled a large piece of steel plate away enough for a body to fit through!

He then perforated with small holes the outside cladding, turned to me and asked "are you coming"? He began kicking the perforated area outwards! I wasn't sure but think I would have gone given the chance, it was not to be though because I heard and felt the van scream to a halt, the jolting halt of the Van threw both of us forward. The door opened and four Officers rushed in grabbed us by arms and pushed us roughly to the floor, swearing and threatening loudly!

They had seen in mirrors and heard the crash as the outside panel was being kicked out. It took minutes to stop the van and get to us. We knew we were in big trouble as they handcuffed us and dragged us to separate mini cells. My hair had been pulled so hard my head hurt my lip was split and bleeding. "Get in there you fucking bastard" I was thrown and kicked forward into the cell steel door slamming shut. I was scared but tried not to show it. An Officer shouted "just wait till we get you bastards to Walton"!

CHAPTER 18

HMP Walton Blues

I was sure I knew what he meant, we were in for a physical beating when we got to Walton! Seeing Walton Gaol for the first time made me feel apprehensive. Arriving at the Prison our transport stopped its engine idling; instructions came loudly over the intercom with military command to the Security Officers in the Meat Wagon. Metal on metal as keys turned, hard steel bolts pulled back and the heavy creaking gates opened. The vehicle inched forward into the dim lit entrance. A voice called the driver to stop and the heavy steel Gates closed behind us. A cold shiver run through my body in the darkness and I took a deep breath.

    Two Officers led me roughly still handcuffed to a white painted brick cubicle, pushed me in telling me in a loud voice "to strip off your clothes don't speak unless spoken to and call all Officers Sir"! A mean faced unsmiling black uniformed guard gave me a dark blue rough cotton prison jacket grey overalls blue striped shirt, vest, underpants, tooth brush, socks blankets, sheets and shoes. Every word from the screws were loudly barked orders. I was ordered to "quick march" everywhere no talking, my photograph was taken then marched to the Doctors office for medical and ordered to strip nude. A man in a doctor's white coat looked in my mouth hefted my testicles ordering me to cough! I was weighed and ordered to put my prison clothes back on, that was it the medical over! I was escorted into a senior guard's office, accompanied by a guard who stood at my side.

The senior guard sat behind a large wooden desk, he had beady eyes a large square stubbly jaw hooked nose, cropped hair and busting beer gut, he looked a real hard case. He stated "he knew I had done a bit" so wouldn't be going into detail, "I'm sure you know the ropes inside, so keep your nose clean and you will do quiet time"! He spoke in an offhand manner like he couldn't care less saying "this is your number" passing me a slip of paper "when addressed you answer to this number, give it when asked, so remember it, now f---k off and don't forget the Sir".

Both me and the other prisoner were put in separate small holding cubicles, where we were told to wait. I knew this was the time I had been dreading! I wasn't wrong minutes afterwards, the door burst open and several prison officers came in so fast I never stood any chance of defending myself, I was slapped punched kicked and dragged. I curled up into a small ball in the corner of the cubicle and endured the beating, until I thought "pretend they have hurt your head" I screamed from behind my hands "my head, my head" they did stop and backed out of the cubicle growling "we'll teach you, you little bastard, damaging prison property you f.....g c....t". The door slammed shut behind them, and I breathed a big sigh of relief! I heard shouts and profanity from the next cubicle, I knew the other prisoner was getting his beating. Then the sound of marching heavy footsteps of the screws as they retreated back to their office. We were bruised and battered, but only we and they ever knew about it!

We accepted this punishment, we knew if we complained, life would become a living hell for both of us so we remained quiet, but we were angry and resentful. The days ahead would heal our bruises but not our animosity towards the Prison Staff. Eventually after what seemed a long time I was marched into the bowels of the Prison Wings area. The smell of cheap disinfectant was everywhere, and at the end of each grey and blue corridor, was a heavy steel painted grey

Diamond in the Stone

barred gate with several large brass heavy locks leading to yet another, everywhere sounded hollow, every sound echoing loudly.

Two guards led me at a march, I was struggling to keep up with my arms full of prison issue kit, Blankets Sheets Pillow slips extra Underwear. I was sore from the beating and in pain but kept up. I knew now how these guards operated and I was being extra careful not to upset them for fear of attracting another beating. After many locked gates along shiny pale blue tiled corridors, we came to a large heavy wooden blue painted door, it too had double brass locks, the Prison staff opened it noisily and I was told to go through...... I saw for the first time the inside of Walton Prison. The door led through to the main wing of the prison 4 landings high, about sixty cells to a landing! 2 prisoners per cell many had three prisoners due to overcrowding.

Narrow iron steps led to each landing. Each landing had steel white rails on each front edge, between each landing was a steel net, stretched from one side to the other, I found out the reasons for the nets later! The loud constant echoing sounds of men's voices, guards barking orders, steel trays rattling, cell doors banging, keys jangling, prisoners shouting to other prisoners from their Cells or out of the barred windows, it was the scary place. I was marched kit in hand to the ground floor Cells. Each cell had a board screwed to the side wall in front of the cell, with the name and number of the prisoners in that cell.

The Cell door was grey painted and steel plated, with a small covered spy hole for Officers to check the occupants inside, or that you were not hanging from the barred windows! The Ground Floor were the New Reception Cells were new prisoners spent the first few days and nights in a Single Cell on constant watch in case of a suicide attempts. The cell was about 6ft wide by 9ft long, with a wooden grey painted corner shelf a steel barred window recessed into the wall, a plastic Piss Pot and one single steel framed bed. The walls were painted a pale white, there was a small brown desk like cupboard with several plastic drawers. The light was recessed into the ceiling with a flat domed cover that giving off a very dim yellowy light...it was grim!

    The door slammed shut behind me making me jump. I dropped my Prison kit on the cold red painted concrete floor and just stood quietly for a while. Even with the Cell door shut I could hear the jumble of echoing voices and sounds, loudest being the slamming of cell doors from each of the steel landings. By the time I had got to my cell after going through Searches Shower Change into Prison Clothing Questions Medical and my Physical Beating it was supper time!

    At supper time my cell door was opened by an Officer who had a Prisoner with him who dished tea into my plastic mug from a large steel Ern that sat on a trolley. The con giving out the tea looked a hard case with a spotty scarred face a muscular physique, close cropped hair mean eyes and a scowl that disfigured his face. The screw barked "right back behind your door" then slammed the heavy door shut. The slamming of many cell doors were like the sounds of echoing gun shots bang bang bang bang on and on! My head throbbed as I sat on the side of the unmade bed my mug of tea in hand comforted by its warmth. I couldn't wait to get into my bed and sleep this nightmare away. Sleep was my escape from a world I'd learned to despise and distrust. The tea was warm weak and insipid; plastic gave the tea a different taste.

CHAPTER 19

HMP Faeces Parcels Galore

I lay on the flat sponge mattress, my feet resting on the neatly stacked sheets and blankets at the end of the bed. Prisoners were not allowed to put bedding on until supper was served. The steel springs below the bed rasped each time I moved position, getting comfortable was next to impossible.

I lay there, looking up at white ceiling with its dull plastic dome covered dull yellow light, with a sense of emptiness wondering what tomorrow would bring? Feeling nothing was a survival tool I had become adept at over the years, my feelings were tucked away somewhere deep inside me where they couldn't hurt me anymore!

The dim light was turned out at 10pm, after a barking order from a Prison Officer assigned to each landing, shouted "lights out" his voice bouncing off every wall in the prison. The Prisoners began calling out to other Prisoners from barred windows. I got to know the sound of a "swinging line" outside the cell window, this was how prisoners passed Tobacco Drugs and Other Stuff to other Prisoners. A Prisoner would take strips of blanket or bed sheet knot them together to make a line, this could be swung from cell to Cell. I learned how some Prisoners pissed off other Prisoners swung "shit parcels" with the promise of Tobacco! How it must have stank on being opened by unsuspecting inmates. I was desperate to have a number two, I was putting it off as it meant sitting on the plastic Piss

River Blue

Pot! And I knew the smell would linger in the cell for ages through the night. The urine and faeces in a plastic pot would become stagnant and stinking by the morning slop out! Throwing the contents out of the window was the norm. And every day the officers would organise a group of inmates with shovels Wellies and bins, would go all around below the cell windows pick up faeces and shit parcels! This was called "the shit parade" and considered a privileged job, because it got you out of your cell into the fresh air!

CHAPTER 20

"Slop Out"

I eventually drifted off wondering what the next day would be like in this hole at 7am....I found out! A bell sounded and a dozen Officers screeching "off your beds and slop out" doors banging keys rattling on each landing in turn. Prison Officers opening and slamming cell doors on each of the six landings, shouting "slop out slop out, make it quick, and back in your cells" My door was opened "slop out you, then back to your cell, come on quickly" I looked out the steel door still in my underpants, it was freezing cold and I wandered where to empty my piss pot. Grabbing my pot, I followed behind a line of other prisoners in various stages of undress cussing swearing and scratching their testicles!

The line led me to the slop out toilet on and middle of the landing. There was a toilet and sink block on each side of the landing, several large white enamel sink troughs with brass taps in each slop out area. The sinks were stained with smelly excrement as each of us in turn tipped out our waste and rinsed our plastic pots and cups! One prisoner a skinny weasel looking con splashed shit accidentally on another prisoner's feet, hell broke loose! Heads butted, fists swung, feet kicked, blood shit and stinking urine splattered the walls! The fighters slipping in Faeces and Urine and the tiled floor began to resemble a Monet painting, it was hellish!

River Blue

Other inmates encouraged them to kill each other, laughing and shouting encouragement. I didn't hang about to see who won! I heard the alarms go off, sound of Officers racing like a mob along the landing to break up the fight.

I was back in my cell by the time the officers were carrying the kicking and swearing Prisoners down the steel stairs to the Solitary Confinement Cell Block in the basement of the prison. Each prisoner was held by Officers hanging on to a limb, one holding the head, two others a leg each, two others holding an arm as the prisoners were carried off to Solitary Confinement five landings down. Whenever I witnessed this happen I couldn't help but admire the Officers who worked together like clockwork, they certainly earned their money in that job! The Officers unfortunately didn't always come away without injury! So this was "slop out" when Prisoners settled scores passed on drugs money alcohol and information.

After returning to my cell, my door was slammed and locked once again until breakfast, again a bell and shouting Officers "unlock for breakfast" I was expected to be ready to leave my cell and make my way to the serving area, grab a tin tray hold it forward for the prisoners dressed in white overalls and white caps to dish breakfast into the tray. They stood serving from behind several gleaming aluminium trolleys, on which stood steaming pots of Porridge hot containers of tea. No inmate was allowed to speak but lots of covert activities took place without the Officers ever knowing, sometimes they did and turned a blind eye! I witnessed a segregated prisoner once on protection from other inmates being beaten while Officers pretended not to see. Prison is a world within a world were normal rules don't always apply, out of sight is out of mind and when out of sight brutal things happen!

CHAPTER 21

Becoming a Prison Baron

After picking up my breakfast, I made my way back to the cell, my door banged once again, ate breakfast, drank my tea and waited until a bang on my cell door woke me as I lay dozing on top of my now stripped bed. It was another prisoner who asked through my cell door spyhole "do you have any tobacco"? I knew better than to give my tobacco away, I had only half ounce of Golden Virginia which I had been allowed to keep as it was purchased from the Isle of Man Prison. But I also knew that if I lent some tobacco out, I could ask twice as much back as interest repayment! This Prisoner was a new and seeing him through the spy hole, he appeared as someone who I could get it back from if push came to shove, so I made a decision to lend a quarter for half ounce back at the end of the week when he got paid. I made sure he fully understood I would not wait for repayment! He understood and agreed. I had taken my first step to becoming a "Baron" which meant I was breaking Prison rules and could get an extra six months on my sentence should I be caught. A lot of violence surrounded "Barons" because some borrowers chose not to pay back, this was serious for both the borrower and the Baron, because if a Baron lost his credibility he would lose his invested output and profit returns. Leading to other borrowers declining to pay back, and those failing to pay back received payback! Directly from the Baron or via a third party contract. Prison rule number 1 "always pay your debts"!

As a new prisoner I was only allocated to a paired cell when it was felt I was not a suicide risk! I waited to be visited by the Senior Officer who eventually turned up about several days later and informed me I would be moving to landing 3 and paired with another prisoner. I was allocated to work in the Screw Shop putting brass screws into electrical plugs six hours a day Monday to Friday and paid about £2.50 a week! On my way to Landing 3 I was greeted by several prisoners who I had met in Institutions along the way.

When I arrived at my new double cell, it was with a guy who I had known from Borstal, he was quiet, but made it known that "his was the bottom bunk", there was "an or else" tone to his voice which I chose to ignore. I don't want to turn this book into another "I was in prison story" needless to say, some days went quietly by just following prison routine, now and again though some crazy things happened! I was there for 5 months and tried to stay out of the Officers way, and avoid trouble.

But it wasn't always possible, on such an occasion I ended up sharing a cell with a man who had mental health problems. He was age about 33 doing 15-year sentence for a very serious crime against a Policeman. I was in a paired cell with him. One night trying to teach him how to play "when the saints come marching in" on the mouth organ he became frustrated with his inability to grasp what I was showing him, he lost it big time and lashed out unexpectedly breaking my nose! I was semi-conscious and bleeding, not knowing what had happened or why, he was towering over me as I regained my senses threatening to "kill me" he was a big strong guy, and I knew he could carry out his threat, so I talked him down, he calmed but I knew I had to get out of there or I would be in danger! The next day I applied for an urgent transfer. I was asked to press charges but I declined. I knew that would bring trouble to my door so I moved cells and life went on. I accumulated a lot of surplus tobacco from my Baron business, but it came with risk, as all breaking of rules did in Prison! One day my cell door was flung open, and several Officers ordered me outside the cell.

Diamond in the Stone

It was a "shake down" I had just the day before taken many ounces of tobacco brand new and Cellophane wrapped from one of my "runners" who did my collections for a fee. It was in my cupboard drawer temporarily, as it was going out in loans this day of my "shake down" I was now standing outside the closed cell door, waiting for the inevitable words "you down the block you're on a charge". This would mean several weeks in "solitary confinement" a further charge, which meant another six months of further Prison time! I was scared, but hid my fear, you can't show fear in a prison, you had to walk tough to survive.

So I waited for the Officers to come out of my cell. They did not find it?? To this day I don't know how they missed a drawer full of tobacco? But they had missed it, I was so relieved but acted slightly irritated by their visit, this was the response expected from me otherwise they may have thought something was out of order! I made a decision that the moment they came out of the cell I was out of the Baron business. I had only several months left to serve, and did not want to spend any more time here than I had to.

I called in all "debts" my business partners did their work and all paid their debts. We changed the Tobacco into money to purchase Alcohol to party just once, big mistake!! Getting tobacco changed into Money or anything else was no small deed in prison, and fraught with risk. Risk of being caught, risk of being" shaken down", risk of being mugged in all sort of ways. So how was it done??...Well we got religious about it, we (my business partners) after much communication / negotiations with bigger tougher men than us, arranged the exchange to be at Church.

The Chapel was a great place, it was full of Prisoners and fewer Officers, an excellent place for all sorts of deals and exchanges to happen, it went like clockwork. We each had a pre agreed amount of tobacco to take to church, it would be exchanged with certain others, who in turn had the goods there and ready to exchange which usually was drugs money and alcohol. Not as easy as it sounds, as all were being watched (allegedly) by Prison Officers.

River Blue

I learned to play guitar, taught by a lifer in for murder. I began to really enjoy reading books, so something positive did come out of Prison I suppose. I left Prison wiser than I went in! Learned to play guitar learned to read and write and how to survive! Like nearly all prisoners leaving prison, I said "I was not going back" but I knew most returned as like me they knew no other way! They had been dragged up rejected and abused. We lived life by the rules we had learned on the streets, in bad sometimes corrupt institutions. I was18 years old without a future!

CHAPTER 22

Changes

When I left Prison I went back to the only place I knew, which was Liverpool. Nothing there had changed and every day was like being that hamster on a wheel sleep bed visit brothers and sisters, go the pub, have a joint, it felt like a depressing and pointless existence.

I suppose the change came after a party in a friend's house, everybody got so drunk a fight broke out and some got badly injured. Alcohol does not agree with me, all I could remember was waking up in another flat bruised and battered, where I was told that a fight had broken out, some had tried to throw me over a landing two stories up! There were threats to injure me badly for days afterwards. I was nervous but on the streets you "pretend" to show fear would lose you "respect" so I hid my fear and resolved to defend myself.

Carrying a weapon became a daily ritual. But I began to think, probably for the first time in my life, of what my options where. If I stayed nobody won and I lost whichever way, I looked at it! Thinking this way led me to believe I did not want this depressing nowhere life. I was 19yrs old and I had nothing, no prospects whatsoever. But I had nowhere to go, I knew nothing except deprivation and the streets. I was going to react as only those growing up in the tough streets of Liverpool can understand which may have ended in violence and a trip back to Prison maybe for a long time! Was I to stay and sort it out? I didn't want to be known as a coward a "divvy" someone who

River Blue

couldn't deal with a situation which needed dealing with! I thought hard and long, probably for the first time in my whole life.

I had an overwhelming knowledge that whatever decision I made would change my life forever for bad or for good! I awoke one morning and decided to leave Liverpool, it was a frightening thought but I wanted to create a life worth living. I had no money and only the clothes on my back! But I had resolved to go and never return! I thumbed a lift from a Haulage Transport Driver who was heading to Birmingham. I had a clean pair of jeans and a top with only the prospect of a homeless existence.

Having grown up "Homeless" it didn't matter! I just knew anything was preferable to the life I was living. The Driver was Liverpool born and bred and a good listener, and we talked a lot on the way to Birmingham. He appeared to understand my dilemma, and suggested he speak to a Manager he knew where he made deliveries, that the guy might know someone with a Job and lodgings for me! I now know the Driver and I were in the right place at the right time.

CHAPTER 23

The Beginning of The End

Arriving in Birmingham, the sun was shining and we stopped at a Supermarket Food Distribution Warehouse in the Black Country in a Town called Dudley. Looking back, I think someone or something was guiding me and the Driver! Because waiting for me was a Job and somewhere to live with the Warehouse Manager! I was miles from anything familiar age19yrs. A Job and a place to live changing my circumstances in a blink of an eye!

It was hard physical work, and a personal battle to discipline myself. Just getting up in the morning was a daily struggle! I had learned to be defensive and aloof over many years and making friends was difficult. My distrust of anybody and everybody made it almost impossible to communicate about anything. So I would turn up and work hard, then bolt for my Apartment room a short walk away until the next day. I had to constantly fight the fear and sense of inadequacy and wore this feeling like a well-worn coat.

Minute by minute, day by day, the urge to return to my comfort zone in the streets of Liverpool plagued me. I did begin to mix a little with some local Afro Caribbean Rasta's with dreadlocks and slip slidy walks, they reminded me of some Liverpool characters I used to know. I liked these cool calm guys who made me laugh with light-hearted banter and we became friends. I was invited to join them at Rasta Night Clubs and Pubs. The first time I showed up at

River Blue

one of their hangouts it scared the life out of me, I had walked in off the street and had to pass two tough smart suited black Bouncers who asked "wat ya want boy"? And stated "dis no place for ya honky" I told them I was looking for some friends and gave the Bouncers their names.

They immediately knew who I was speaking of and directed me up several stairs to a darkened flashing strobe lighted area with loud Bob Marley reggae music drowning out all other sound. This made understanding two Dreadlock Rasta's at the top of the stairs who asked "hey blood man, watcher do here rasclot? dis is de underside whitey, ya go sum other jive man" I decided then I was going home, but a face I knew with a big smile and slip slidy walk called out to me "hey scouse, micky man, watch doin, inya cum man" it was George my Warehouse work colleague.

He led me towards the throbbing ear popping happy Marley Reggae music, green and yellow lights where moving haphazardly over the walls and dance floor. A sea of heaving Black bodies were dancing rhythmically to the cool sounds. The DJ called out poetic words his mouth so close to the microphone, I thought he might swallow it! I was the only white man there! Many eyes…all looking at me, I just wanted to get out of there but George had other plans! "c'mon micky man ye have a drink wid Georgie boy, ye be aright…enjoy da music man" I followed to a dark corner at the back of the room, a group of Rasta young men and woman looked up smiling, "cum man, ye be aright" I was handed a drink, it was rum and coke, still standing I said "cheers man" taking a large swig, which immediately made my whole body glow and vastly reduced the anxiety I had been feeling.

We all were trying to speak, but the music made conversation impossible, so we smiled and nodded a lot. I began to relax, even found myself making small hip and shoulder movements to the music which appeared to amuse my new friends, who laughed and slapped their fingers together giving me thumbs up signs!

I noted a smell pungent and sweet "was it whacky"? I asked. George replied "ye man cum share de peace pipe, make ya dance really

Diamond in the Stone

good" I found myself holding the most enormous cone shaped splif! I drew the smoke deep into my lungs choked and spluttered "white man not use ta good weed, dis good man, keep ya laughing all night" we all fell about laughing uncontrollably, the room appeared to be gently spinning, the music caressed my mind and body. I was floating in a sea of Black smiling faces and bodies, the smell of sweat weed and alcohol the lights and music pulsating! I was totally relaxed enjoying it all...new friends' music clubs.

I discovered later though there was a down side i.e. the money needed and the mood swings the whacky produced, it left me feeling edgy and annoyed at nothing. For the first weeks being stoned became a familiar feeling to me, I wanted to be high! The job wasn't enough to pay for it though! I decided to take a trip back to Liverpool. I told my Rasta friends "I could get good weed cheaper than in Birmingham, they all chipped some money in. A was given a lift from a new friend who loved the whacky, and got me to the door of a Pusher in the back streets of Parliament Street in Liverpool where weed was grown like grass "literally"!

I had discovered this place while on the run from the Children's Homes. The pusher was a skinny gaunt pale faced man about thirty something, with beady sly eyes. He answered the door and in a thick nasal scouse accent he asked us "what we wanted"? "Were looking for weed man" he smiled, teeth stained brown "come you've come to the right place" We followed him into a room filled with the familiar pungent aroma of weed. A record player and giant speakers dominated the room, it was nicely furnished, he was making money if the expensive furniture was anything to go on. I noted some movement in a back room, this was probably his back up against a shake down or robbery by those he sold to. "How much ye want man" I asked suspiciously "how much an ounce" he pulled open a drawer in the large coffee table, producing the biggest bag of green buds I had ever seen, the smell increased a 100 fold.

A pair of gold scales where used to portion out an ounce "that's an ounce, ye want it? Will cost ye" this was great, I had the money

25% of mine and 75% belonged to my Rasta friends. I said "that's ok weigh me a bag" He weighed out my deal, we were happy with the amount. I wanted to know how good it was, so asked him to roll up a joint we could try, it took me and my companion into a euphoric state were nothing mattered, it was good stuff, my Rasta friends would be pleased and I would earn some profit for myself...

Life felt good as we drove high as kites back to Birmingham listening to Marley and Rock music, singing all the way to Moody Blues, the Beatles, Dylan and David Bowie occasionally stopping to skin up and to take a leak. Life felt good, I was about to make some easy money (or so I thought) actually life was about to get very scary! I had decided to short deal my Rasta friends and make a little extra cash for myself. This was to go badly wrong! George my Rasta friend arrived early evening at my flat "were da stuff man, bin waiting for ya nice weed fa me money" I gave him a polythene bag filled with green sun dried marijuana buds, the bag didn't stop the sweet sickly smell of weed, it was overpowering... "Its good stuff man, you will love it" he sniffed at it hefted the bag in his big meaty black hand and said "man, ya pissing wid me, da deal is short" my heart thumped in my chest, I knew there was going to be serious trouble. Street rule number (1) "you don't mess with the weed! I had taken a few quid's worth out of the deal, I had given to him! "hey come on man, weigh it" he demanded... "ye got scales man" I told him "no, just food scales, but he was welcome to weigh it at his place"

I was bluffing and blagging what else could I do? He snatched the bag saying "I be back man" in a menacing threatening slow unsmiling drawl. He left, I breathed a sigh of relief, but as soon as he weighed it, he would be back, I would be under serious threat to limb and life. At 10pm that evening several hours later, a hard banging knock came at my door, my heart raced once again...opening the door three Black men, one being George looked serious and didn't wait to be asked in! George my Rasta friend stated "ye mess wid de wrong f.. kers man, bad deal, it weighed short, na ye pay us man" trying to stay cool I said "listen man, I have some scales let's just see shall we" while they were away that evening and expecting them to return I had recalibrated the scales in the kitchen. I put their bag on the scales praying silently that this would work...the weight was exactly right! They each picked the bag up placing it back on the scales, "man ya lucky boy ya know" they left scratching their heads and speaking street to each other! I acted offended saying "after this, don't ever ask me to do you a favour again" and shut the door. I smiled, a smile they never saw! Relief washed over me, I settled down and skinned up, what a night! I remember to this day that I was about to get seriously injured that night, the Angels must have been watching over me, on top of some quick thinking and action, an extra few quid nearly cost me dearly! And to boot they were my friends and felt guilt probably for the first time in my life, they deserved better.

CHAPTER 24

A Prayer Answered

And it was in Birmingham several weeks later that I had the darkest day of my life. I began to feel depressed, everything felt black and hopeless. I had struggled with these feelings all my young life, but this was a feeling of absolute worthlessness, a dark night of my soul and felt I did not want to live anymore! I suspected smoking a lot of wacky had a hand in my depressed state of mind. I had nothing to live for. No more struggling day to day seemed more desirable to me than ever. I had witnessed several suicides in Prison, guys who weren't here anymore, maybe I too would be better off dead? I felt I had no value, nothing to give. I had reached my limit, no more of this shit life. I could not see anything in life worth the day to day struggle of survival. I cried from deep within me for help and helped I was!

CHAPTER 25

Searching

I needed to find somewhere I could learn about my answered prayer. I visited many Churches without finding what I was seeking. I learned about the "Born Again" the Jehovah's Witnesses Protestants Catholics Baptists found good people in all of them but none resonated with my answered prayer! I kept looking reading everything I could find on the subject of conversion and spiritual awareness.

In the mean time I continued to go to work in a steel foundry, spraying a wet mix of enamel onto giant mixing containers for ICI, which when into furnaces to baked the sprayed powder into glass. I hated the job, I coughed up blue dust most days and nights, as the protective garments and ventilation masks where not efficient. I was informed that the foundry had become a "closed shop" i.e. if you refused Union membership you could be dismissed, this I thought couldn't be right.

I fought against joining until an ultimatum was given me by the higher management, join or leave! Every week men were having accidents due to poor unsafe working conditions, so thinking, "If you can't beat them, join them" maybe try to get some unsafe practices changed. A shop steward was needed (AEUW) for our spray and furnace factory, I applied and got the badge. Passionate about health and safety issues was not enough, it was expected that the union rep speaks up at meetings where sometimes 40 men hung on every word. I felt terrified and froze several times in mid-sentence, so embarrassing, I was filled with fear! Why? I did not know, but I couldn't keep pretending, public speaking was not my thing.

I found out that although the men working there with me would moan and groan and complain about this and that, when it came to supporting me at meetings, they were silent, in fear of losing their jobs. I was 19 years old, did I really want to spend my life in an iron foundry? No! I had seen several men either retire or just not return to work after becoming so ill, but what was I to do? I had no skills, little experience in anything! So I stuck at it, bored and frustrated. Hating every minute, but needing the small wage to pay my bills.

One day though I had a wonderful experience. I had read a short poem about flowers and trees, the beauty to be found in all things, it left me wondering, where? Why couldn't I see what the poet was seeing? It baffled my mind, if he could see such beauty, why not me? For many days it bothered me. So one day I decided on my hour lunch break, I would slip outside behind the furnace, which was a piece of waste ground, mostly covered in weeds and cinders from the furnace, pools of brown stagnant water here and there. I determined that, if the poet had the same eyes as me, I must be able to see beauty too!! I picked up a cinder about the size of a golf ball; it was rough and had the appearance of molten lava, with holes and sharp edges, it was wet, still dripping from the pool, I had picked it out from. I found a comfortable bit of old red brick broken wall, sat and stared at this chunk of cinder for ages, it appeared ugly, dirty, grey, sharp and jagged. So where was the beauty? I kept looking concentrating very hard, searching out each minute detail, its texture, colour, shape.

I could see nothing but an old piece of molten rock! Looking even harder, suddenly I saw small swirls of colour in the cracks and crevices of the lava, there was blue, red, green, purple, yellow, and the light from the sky was reflecting glistening sparkles of light, like diamonds, specks of light that within them appeared as small rainbows, the colours were luminous, the grey had turned to silver, the lava stone felt alive in my hand, my mind was filled with a sense of wonder at the beauty of this common piece of melted rock. I had seen it, the beauty with my own eyes, the poet was right, it was amazing.

I now know the secret. We look, but don't see! We listen, but don't hear! Have hearts that don't feel! Why? Because we don't allow our full intention and attention! Our minds are filled with occupying thoughts and fears of day to day survival. Learning this simple but life changing lesson, means I give, whatever I do my full attention, especially nature and living things. The beauty of the moment is illuminated into an inspiring event! My senses come alive and constantly amazed. I'm no more special than you. I thought the poet was using "poetic licence" no, he was pointing me to the "gift" which is in each and every moment. Jesus said "what good a gift if a man receives it not" why did it take so long for me to find this gift? Because it was hidden in plain sight! I realised I had been searching in all the wrong places! I now knew what Jesus meant when he said "the kingdom of heaven is within", "seek ye first the kingdom of heaven and all these things will be added unto you".

CHAPTER 26

I Found My Life and Future

The beauty I saw in that piece of burned Cinder left me with the impression that my mind was not who I really was! There was a whole unseen world inside and outside which I wanted to explore find and experience. My survival depended on earning a living but something inside of me had changed for the better. I had a sense of purpose, and urge to do better things, to give to others. These feelings and thoughts I'd never experienced before. I was not going to waste any more of my life on conditioned emotions and behaviours that had been reinforced, by a Society structured and controlled by corporate interests that influence every aspect of all our lives. I believe Religion Politics Finance Science and Education enable control of the masses, and orchestrated far in advance all Wars, and separation of people across the Globe!

In my early awakening I thought to gain understanding by studying Religion but the responses I got from their leaders left me in no doubt that their Religions were scripted to support the Social order narrative! A small, plump Irish Priest began telling me of the hell and damnation, I would receive if I strayed from the narrative emphasising the need to obey! I visited several Churches each giving their version of obedience to a vengeful God! I had experienced hidden beauty which was happening more and more, when I gave full attention to my inner sight.

I eventually gave up seeking knowledge from Religions! But I had a deep desire to truly experience life to make my life worth living. I took up a Volunteers post in a Hospital giving out tea and coffee on a designated ward. I probably would not get an opportunity like this today with all the PC entrenched into our English culture. I loved my work on the ward. I experienced real people in life and death situations. I witnessed Courage Sadness Grief Pain and Suffering. All of us are amazing! I felt a deep compassion and willingness to assist. I loved every minute of every day and was first in and last out always.

Never before had I felt so alive. I felt useful doing something worthwhile, my mind was no longer on my past and was very much in each moment. I cried with relatives, held hands with the suffering, helping where ever I was needed. I worked for nothing picking up Unemployment Benefit which wasn't enough to eat healthily. I discovered that I could get a free meal and a drink each day as a Voluntary worker and the Hospital food was the best I had ever tasted, and always plentiful. In the Canteen I met many full time workers of the Hospital- Doctors, Nurses Teachers all good people. One day after Volunteering at the Hospital for 8 months, I met Director of Nursing Mr B. He was a well-spoken educated man. We spoke on a few occasions and I liked him a lot. One day he said to me "Why don't you become a Nurse"? Just like that! Me a Nurse! A Nurse! I was speechless. How could an uneducated person like me be a Nurse? All Nurses I had met where educated and spoke good English. Me a Nurse!?

He must have read my mind; the next words he spoke send me into a world I could not have dreamt of. He said "go to College get 5 O Levels and I will guarantee you a Nurse Training Placement"! My mind could not conceive or imagine learning anything, and no one I knew had 5 O levels! He was asking a lot! At school I couldn't take anything in, sent to a "Special School" for slow learners which had reinforced my sense of inadequacy! My mind told me "don't bother your stupid"! I explained to Mr B how I felt, he just said "try your best and you will succeed, then come and see me"!

For the next several weeks I battled with my conditioned mind. How could this man who knew my back ground and circumstances have so much faith in me? I had never been encouraged before in my life. Mr B told me in later conversations that he had been watching me with interest over the months as I had worked at the Hospital, he had noted my compassionate enthusiasm and reliability at work, that I "would make a damn good Nurse". Could I do it?

CHAPTER 27

My Education

I dragged my feet on the issue of Education until I met a School Teacher called Barbara, she and her family, changed my life for ever and was Heaven sent. We met as a result of a knock on my door one dark stormy wet night. I was sitting in alone about 8 pm in a small house I had rented near Bilston.

A knock on my door surprised me as the weather outside was so bad, so the chance of anyone calling would be unlikely. Opening the front door, I was shocked to find two young men dressed in dark suits shirt and ties. A large badge on their lapel announcing them as Missionary Elders from the Church of Jesus Christ and Latter Day Saints! They were both soaked through and I felt concerned for them.

They looked me straight in the eye announcing very confidently, that they "had a message for me personally and felt inspired to knock on my door to give me the message"!! Curious and intrigued I asked them in offering them towels and a cup of tea or coffee. They declined a Coffee or Tea explaining in American accent "they did not drink either, but a cup of Chocolate would be nice if I had any"? it so happened I did have and made it piping hot for them as they towelled themselves dry. They told me "I was a son of a Heavenly Father who loved me and would begin to behold the many wonders of living, if I learned to love my Father and all on earth".

It hit me with such intensity at the time that for the next 28 years I would strive to do just that. I was Baptised several weeks later. I had read and studied the whole of The Book of Mormon, and it was ages before they asked me to be Baptised. It was then I met Barbara the School Teacher who encouraged me to get educated with the words "just try your best and you will succeed"! Both her and Mr B had given me the same message!

So with courage I was going to try. I enrolled in night classes at the local School to try get an English Literature O Level. I went for several months then sat the test. I tried so hard and enjoyed doing so, but felt silly as all the other students where younger than me, being sixteen and seventeen. I thought they were all much cleverer than me, and often left the class feeling discouraged. Each time I would talk to Barbara who encouragingly said "keep at it". I sat the Exam and waited expectantly for the result, it came back Unmarked? I'd been so nervous I had only finished half the Exam! It knocked me right off my feet. I decided to give up on education. But my friend Barbara said "try again, but this time go to College" what? me College! My mind once again was my enemy telling me "don't bother, you will fail, you are stupid" but each time Mr B and Barbara's words came back to me encouraging me to try my best. Then I read a Scripture from the Bible which said that answers would come to me" I believed these words that I would be helped. I enrolled part time evening College signing up for 5 O levels!

My enrolment date was to be half way through the education year. I did not want to wait that long, so speaking with the Head of the College we agreed I could commence immediately, he cautioned me not to expect to pass anything in six months, but enjoy getting to know the subjects which would prepare me for next year's exams! What! 18 months, before I could sit the Exams! No way!

I really believed I would be successful so I determined I had six months to prepare to sit all 5 examinations! And study I did. I set myself a daily time table of relevant reading material targeted at my subjects English Language. Biology. Sociology. English Literature and Art. I worked my Voluntary hours at the Hospital, then go to the College library and studied until my eyes hurt and head ached. I took every opportunity to learn, sitting extra classes every chance I got. I even decided to do an A level in Art because I enjoyed it so much. Then 6 months later the week of the exams came. I sat each one in turn.

One English Literature exam I was half hour late getting there, the examiner said just "do your best, you can always sit it again next year" no way! I had worked hard and was ready, I would just write my answers faster!

I did, and finished ahead of everyone in the Exam and was the only one to get a top mark!! The answers to all the Exams just flowed from my mind! It was amazing and wonderful.

I was not stupid after all! I passed every exam including an A Level in half the time allotted, I felt amazing! I was proud of myself for my hard work and commitment. My faith in a force outside of myself grew by mega amounts, proud for the first time in my life since bringing home chicken bones from the bins! I ran over to Barbara's house to give her the good news, I felt like I could fly! She was over the moon and congratulated me for all my efforts and success.

CHAPTER 28

A Nurse!

I took my results to Mr B in the school of Nursing, he too was amazed that I had achieved so much in six months and couldn't praise me enough. True to his word, I was given my Nurse Application papers, and was on the Registered Nursing course within 3 months! My RGN training lasted 3 years and gave me so much. My confidence mushroomed, I gained knowledge, greater compassion and many opportunities to learn and grow as a person. I was the only male in a class of thirty students to begin with. Several exams followed after each Nursing placement on the wards and in the community. I loved every minute of each of those hard wonderful days. Every time I felt down or discouraged I would look into the sky at the Aeroplanes flying overhead, thinking to myself, "one day I will go anywhere in the world" and I have!!

I loved Nursing and the feelings I got from helping others, getting paid was a bonus and unexpected pleasure. In Church I became an Elder and High Priest, a Sunday school teacher, a priesthood leader of a new branch of the church. I learned to socialise with good and honest people. Public speaking to large audiences in church was terrifying at first, then I learned to love it and I took every opportunity to do so. My faith in a power outside of myself enabled me to give my best and all my days have proved it to be so!

Whilst Nursing I began to feel like a worthwhile person, I felt it was a privilege to be a Nurse giving my best and all to those entrusted to my care. I knew from day one that the quality of the lives in my care where in part dependent on my attitude and skills. Becoming a Nurse for me as my younger years had conditioned me not to care. I had to resolve this conditioning if I was to truly care! I wanted to feel like a person who could be relied on, one who was willing to help any who needed help and I have striven to be such a person.

Nobody could see the battle going on with in me. I was once told "act like the person you want to be, and eventually you become that person". So true I now know! So how was I as a Nurse? I was amazing! I loved my profession, and worked to be the best, to give my best, and have been rewarded in so many ways both as a person and materially ever since. Am I a good person now? I believe I am, but being so is still a constant 24/7 battle. I have all the usual human traits and strongly aware of these faults. My life's ambition and intention is to rise above any traits that would harm another. I accept I'm human no better, no worse than any other. I like myself and proud of the challenges I have faced. Some challenges I have failed; others I have triumphed over. I see life as a great adventure, wonderful and amazing.

CHAPTER 29

My Arthur Daley Smart Suit

Whilst Nursing, I noticed some very smart suited young men and ladies who visited the Hospital from time to time. They dressed well, held mobile phones and briefcases, and drove new cars. I stopped one or two and asked what their jobs where, "Medical/ Pharmaceutical Sales Representatives" They told me of the rewards and the challenges they faced ensuring their products where the ones used in all relevant medical establishments, wow, I thought, "I could do that" so I watched out for vacancies in the medical journals.

My first Interview for a Sales Representative position was like a fairy tale! Magical in fact! I had never worn a suit in my life, but this Interview I purchased an off the peg light grey large lapel double breasted suit from Owen Owen's department Store, a white shirt and blue tie. I turned up at the interview on time and very nervous. My mouth was dry and my palms sweaty. I felt totally out of my depth, but had done my homework and felt I could answer any questions they may ask. I wanted the chance to make a better salary whilst remaining connected to medicine and Nursing. When the Secretary in the Reception area called me in I straightened my back, said a silent prayer and walked in, trying to portray what I hoped was a confident can do person. The Interview was made up of three very smart looking people sitting behind a long dark oak desk. I wanted to

run back out the door. I stood looking from one to the other until the smartest looking and only man on the panel, said "Please take a seat"
    I sat, not knowing whether to cross my legs, fold my arms or what! I sat facing all three willing myself to relax. The smart intelligent looking man spoke first "Well, please let me introduce you to the panel, then maybe I can tell you a bit about our company, then you can tell us about yourself" he was smiling and I warmed to him immediately. He introduced himself as the CEO of the company, introduced his Senior Sales Director then the Sales and Marketing Manager. The two ladies didn't bat an eye lid, just stared at me I felt they did not like me at all!

    Both Ladies were in their thirties and nodded with a tight lipped smile! I told myself "get a grip" the ladies where scary hard looking people and I knew they were going to drill me; I just knew it! The CEO spoke with a refined educated English accent and warm sincerity. He outlined his company products financial status and challenges. I tried to look interested and nodded occasionally, like I knew what the hell he was talking about! Then the moment I was dreading arrived, my tongue stuck to my mouth, my heart beat a little faster and I was hoping that I could speak confidently…

    "So, that's us and the company, can you tell us a little about yourself, and why you have applied for the position in Medical Sales" …pause, gulp, it felt like forever before I was able to speak! I told myself "be yourself and to hell with it" courage came to my rescue. I told them about my journey to becoming a Nurse, how I had seen Medical Pharmaceutical Representatives in the Hospital and my impressions of them, that I had a desire to be smart and successful just like them, "but needed a start in a successful company to prove myself, and believed I would be good at it".

    The CEO smiled, the ladies just looked not impressed! Here it comes and the ladies grilling began, "where did you hear of our company? What do you know about the company? What makes a good Representative"? And many more questions which I answered as best I could, my palms where sweating, sweat trickling down from my arm pits! These ladies appeared not to like me much but at least, I would know what to expect in future interviews. The last question absolutely floored me! It was a question of mathematical percentages of quarterly sales volumes and productivity! What! I didn't have a clue of what they were talking about! Couldn't even begin to answer them or where to start! I went numb with fear, I did not know the answer! I was an idiot to think I could be like those guys at the Hospital in suits and briefcases, they had Degrees and posh backgrounds! I told myself "well at least I tried" then suddenly and unexpected, the CEO broke into the grilling "Can I ask you a personal question? I hope you won't be offended" I responded slightly nervously that "whatever he asked I would try to answer"

I knew what was coming, he was going to ask me why I had bothered to apply! I was so relieved to get off the hook from answering the last question from the Managers phew! The ladies now looked perplexed as to why the CEO intervened before they got the answer to the killer question? Just when she was about to put the boot in! The CEO had held up his hand looking in her direction as if to say "OK, that's enough" he then asked his question, a question I would not have expected in a million years! He asked "where did you get that suit?"

I was gob smacked stunned and relieved and replied "Owen Owen's" he smiled his warm smile and said "you look a little like Arthur Daily" we both laughed, the ladies slightly smiled also as not to show disrespect for the CEO's joke! To me they were asking themselves "What's the suit got to do with whether he can do the job"? He and I had genuinely laughed changing the atmosphere. I liked this man, he was human with a sense of humour. But then things got stranger. He asked "If I offer you the job, will you change that suit? If you accept and agree, I will take you to lunch then to my personal Tailor and get you measured up" just like that! This man had power and was using it, the ladies where stunned, their faces said it all! Looking at the CEO I replied "of course I will accept the position and agree to change my suit, I don't like it either" both he and I laughed again! I had been given the job I thought was so above me, never expecting to get into the Industry at first interview! The unseen force was with me again, there could be no other explanation of such a wonderful outcome. The CEO took me to lunch and had me measured for Suit shirt and matching tie! Then he took me to a Car Showroom and asked me to choose a car, with in a price range of course! I did and it was delivered to my home several days later!

CHAPTER 30

Follow The Money

And so began my next adventure and learning opportunity! It had all happened like a dream but even dreams contain challenges and I had many. I had Cycled 26 miles a day while training as a Nurse for several years then purchased a Moped for the last 12 months, then drove a second-hand Ford car after completing my RGN successfully.

My Driving test took me three attempts before I passed! You can imagine I was a bit nervous finding myself 2 years later driving a brand new top of the range car! As a Medical Sales Representative I spent many hours and miles driving up and down motorways, speaking to Doctors Nurses Supplies Managers and Surgeons.

In the very second week after my initial sales and product training, I forgot to put the handbrake on whilst parked on a hill, it was my worst nightmare! The brand new shiny car was pointing downhill and before I realised, the shiny new car had begun to roll without me in it! The car gathered speed me running behind it in pursuit, willing it to stop! It stopped with its pointy end buried deep into the back of another car a hundred yards down the road. I took the details and left a note under the windscreen wiper of the unfortunate owner! I was able to get the companies car to a nearby garage.

I called my Manager who was the dragon on the interview panel! She stated scornfully "you left the handbrake off a brand new car"?? Her tone and words told me that I was an idiot, who should never have been set loose with such a nice shiny object! Informing me she would be speaking to the CEO, oh no it just kept getting worse! I felt once again this job was too big for me!

As it turned out however I was very successful my enthusiasm tenacity and hard work paid off in Sales Growth! I worked on the numbers knowing that the more people I spoke to about the products, the more hospitals supplies departments and Nurses would order our products.

I was well rewarded and enjoyed the challenge of increasing the company's profits and my own bank balance! I noted after several years that there where Global Company Pharmaceutical Representatives whose rewards and salaries were much higher than mine! I was looking for more challenge and greater rewards. I was becoming obsessed with making money! Once again going after what I believed was beyond me, but I had learned a real truth, that nothing was impossible if I tried hard enough! I felt a Higher Power was always with me, especially when the fear was real!

CHAPTER 31

Ambition

I began asking high end Pharmaceutical Sales Representatives I met around where the best Career positions were? I was advised that I would need more than a couple of years' experience and success. This frustrated me somewhat as I wanted to get straight up on that big horse.

One day whilst hanging about in a Hospital Cafe, I met a Representative that told me about a young company with a very interesting and new product. The company had been set up by a Father and Son. The son was a Doctor and had spotted a niche in the Wound Dressings Market they had sold their homes and invested every penny into Clinical Research and manufacture of a Natural Organic plant into an effective Wound Care product. It had received approval and licence and were seeking a Sales Force to take it out to potential users such as Surgeons Nurses and Doctors. It sounded amazing and was a first for this type of product.

It turned out to be a multimillion pound market and made the company 22 Million Pounds in a buyout by a Global Company after only three years! I was taken on by this Global company, and within a year had the highest sales of the product in my territory. So one year after joining the Company I was promoted to be Executive Sales Trainer which messed with the heads of many of the old timers, who were resentful of my promotion, me a new comer who didn't even have a degree! Several of the Representatives resigned. They had forgotten the golden rules of Numbers and tenacity! I loved the job and the extra cash purchased renovated and sold three houses as the housing market was booming at that time. I felt career wise it was becoming repetitive and unchallenging!

CHAPTER 32

Reaching for The Sky

So what did I do, I looked for a bigger job with more money and rewards! I wanted to travel, so once again with my eyes and ears open I spotted an advertisement in the Times for an International Business Development Manager!

I was shaking when I read the advert, but by this time shaking only served to challenge me. I knew I could get the job, but wasn't sure I could do the job! A well written CV a sharp suit, and company background research made me feel very confident on the day of the interview and I got the job! Little did I know just what a challenge this Position would be. The money was amazing with expense account and car. I drove a top of the range Mercedes; this was my dream job or so I thought!

In between success and going after money, my family of two beautiful teenage daughters and long suffering wife were getting further and further away! Although materially better off my family seldom saw me, when they did I was tired and exhausted most of the time, away from home for several weeks at a time. The dream was turning into a nightmare!

CHAPTER 33

Money Rich Time Poor

When I did have free time, it was taken up by my Church responsibilities. I had been ordained a Priest, then High Priest and given responsibilities as a leader in the Church. My wife felt neglected and threatened that she would leave with the children if I did not pay more attention to our family and their needs!

My wife did leave at one point which was my wakeup call. I begged her forgiveness, promised I would change things, give them my attention. I felt under tremendous stress. I gave up my responsibilities in the church. My job was also taking its toll on my health because of stress levels. My responsibilities where many, and time appeared limited. At 35 I began noticing more and more grey hairs appearing.

I was coming to the realisation that money was not everything, my family life got better, but my tiredness was constant. I needed to switch off time and space to relax. I did my best to put on a brave face but the pressure was showing often irritable there was always more to do! The year it came to a head, I was made redundant from my position as International Business Manager, after the company lost several large contracts.

I felt very low at this point, so decided to use the time off to purchase another rundown property in an exclusive area. I knew a large amount of work would have to be done if I was to make the investment payoff foolishly deciding this was just what I needed.

River Blue

I worked from morning to evening, knocking down, building, landscaping, extending upwards, outwards and decorating for several months.

I was exhausted physically and mentally, within three months, I had given the House a new character and significantly increased the value a great deal. Not bad for three months work I thought! But I also noted, that with so much time spent on the house, my wife and children were once again taking a back seat.

When I look back now, I realise just how driven towards success and money I had become. After completing the house project, we decided to take a break in Switzerland, so off we went. It was a disaster and shook my world, which came tumbling down! I returned home from the break abroad alone, on the surface my outward appearance was normal. I appeared in control, but it was a mask hiding much emotional pain. Inside I was desperately unhappy, a deep sense of rejection was overwhelming me. My pride was the main problem, great anger swelled up in me because of feeling rejected.

I couldn't see it at the time, but I had regressed to the child rejected by parents and reacting to what I imagined was that same rejection. I apportioned the blame to everyone else but myself. What a fool I was tricked by my own egotistical mind and unresolved Childhood issues. I did not realise that unresolved past issues can impact on present day circumstances. Deep emotional pain can claw their way to the surface. I know now that now. If buried emotions are not confronted bravely with compassion, forgiveness and letting go, those emotions can disrupt every good thing in one's life.

For several years I tried desperately to resurface, crying out silently to that unseen power, which had helped me so many times before, but was pulled under by invisible forces.

I learned at this time, that my Son had died of an overdose of a Controlled drug, which had probably been mixed with a bulking agent so as to give the Dealer greater profit! He had managed, I was told to dial 99 on his mobile in an effort to save himself, but was found dead the next day…The news left me in a state of shock, and tears like rain fell for days and weeks.

The pain was overwhelming, I screamed in my mind at God, then slammed the door and bolted it, so tight that no light could enter. What does one do when all one holds sacred suddenly disappear from your life? I went into the world of distractions, the illusions of happiness played out in all the world.

CHAPTER 34

Searching

I had not drunk Alcohol smoked or frequented bars since age 20 I was now age 49. I had been married over 28 years, and thought I could lose myself in distractions. I changed jobs wanting to get back to caring in some way.

I volunteered my services to the Prison Services, knowing my juvenile years spent in institutions had given me an insight into the mind-set of those imprisoned. I imagined I could motivate others who had similar circumstances to my own. My service was accepted after speaking with the Prison Governor, telling him of my past as an offender and experience of broken family life, Foster Homes, Juvenile Centres, Detention Borstal and Prisons and my journey back to the surface.

He encouraged me to take on a full time position in the Rehabilitation Team, which consumed my life for the next 6yrs. going into the Prison to work was a nerve racking experience, like walking back into my past! The past I had tried so hard to leave behind swearing never to return! What was I doing? But here I was back in a Prison again climbing cold steel steps to the Prison Cells. It sent chills down my spine for the first three months, my first days back in this dark rancid Prison atmosphere was overwhelming.

The dull artificial lighting, smell of disinfectant, body odours, noises of slamming steel doors, raised voices of Prison officers yelling,

Diamond in the Stone

"get behind your doors, slop out" it was like stepping back into a nightmare, my mind screamed at me to "get out of there". Memories of a past life events filled my mind. The sense of my own fear was overwhelming, so much so, that several times in the first week, I contemplated calling it a day and getting a million miles away from there! But the old familiar shaking and nervousness strengthened my resolve to finish what I had set out to do. Prisoners stared at me, some making sarcastic comments, and giving me arrogant looks as I climbed the stairs and walked the landings orientating myself to this hostile environment.

I told myself over and over, "stick with it, there might be someone just like me someone who could benefit from my insights into getting out of the mire of circumstances and wrong choices". I saw it as a mission to find any who were truly lost. Those with broken childhoods, those who had never experienced love or affection, those who were following the herd into the slaughter house of life. I was in for some big surprises, and reality checks in the days to come. I felt I had re-entered a jungle. I knew from experience what I was going to encounter here. I prepared myself, revisiting in my mind, the characters I had encountered in my earlier journey through institutional life. The violent minded, manipulators psychiatric illness sufferer's wheelers and dealers plus the crude rude arrogant professional criminals. Gang member's racists and junkies, and they were all there!

But, it didn't faze me, I had been there, knew how life worked for the inmates! A world with in a world with rules that attracted penalties, punishments and rewards. New inmates had to learn the ropes, and it was pass or fail! The Prison officers, the "screws" had their world, and maintained control via penalties, punishments and rewards also. I knew every trick in the book from past experiences, and would implement this understanding to try and help, thinking "if I could find the lost ones, I could help them".

Finding "them" proved very hard, nearly all had intentionally broke the law for gain and street wise. For six years I searched, I am not sure to this day whether I made a difference to anyone's life for the better. For 6 years I worked to find the Prisoners Housing Education Business start-up grants Drug Support Jobs and DWP assistance. After the Offenders left Prison feedback was poor, and I never knew if those assisted ever remained free for long, my heart hopes.

CHAPTER 35

Too Much to Bear

An experience one day whilst working at the Prison left me traumatised, a new Prisoner I was interviewing, turned out to be a Drug Dealer (class A) he was cocky brash and arrogant. He bragged in street talk about "his boys" and his "wealth" gained from the sale of class A drugs, making the statement "some users die, their choice man" The words sank deep to my core and left me feeling physically sick......I had to request to leave the interview drained by the experience. I left the Prison for several weeks of bereavement counselling. The grief for my Son had been the cause of my reaction, I didn't want to return but did. I had responsibility on return to support a Serial Paedophile who was due to be released.

I was not allowed to show my feelings and each interview left me drained and physically sick. During the interviews the man aged about 36 spoke of his Paedophile activities with no remorse! He had been used as a Child, and thought it was rational and normal to have sexual feelings for children!? Whilst trying to gain accommodation for several Prisoners due to leave, it was hard to gain information from other departments, to support my applications for Housing! I became disillusioned. Before leaving I received a Nomination from the Prisoners for a Justice Department Award of recognition. I proudly received it from the Prison Governor but I knew my mission at the Prison was over.

CHAPTER 36

The Path to My Enlightenment

While working at the prison I met a lady who became my wife, she introduced me to "Meditation" which has proved another turning point. I have practiced daily Meditation since 2011 which has led to some fascinating experiences, the greatest being Peace and Out of Body Travel.

Looking back on my life I see that each day from birth has been a challenging and learning journey. I've studied the words of Jesus and Biblical texts some of which left me perplexed as to the words meanings. Words such as "be still" and "the kingdom of Heaven is within" … "I am the way the truth and the light" … "the first will be last and the last shall be first" and that in the last days the Earth would be transformed with a "new Earth and new Heavens" … "men would beat swords into ploughshares" and the "Lion would lay down with the lamb"! I could not grasp the meaning then, but I now know what these and many words meant. Could it be, Jesus was a Meditator also? (Forty Days and Nights in the Dessert) And knew the direction the Earth? ("A New Earth and New Heavens") its inhabitants where heading? We are now in a time when a few control the many. The wealth of the planet has been absorbed into Global Corporate groups bloodlines and Royalty, who control the Money the Banks Media Pharmaceuticals Arms Industries and Governments. The Deep State Covert Representatives of Governments decide who lives and who dies! Crimes are disguised as legitimate Wars by powerful Puppet Masters for profit and power. Innocents are slaughtered for their profit and greed for power. The controlled News Media and Movie messages manipulate the emotions of the masses, to gain support for the murder of innocents.

And this situation Jesus spoke of and believed that these inhuman acts would be visited by Justice. Slavery still exists and we are as much slaves now as the Israelites! All generations before and after have been enslaved by the hidden hand behind the curtain!

We have the appearance of freedom! But we cry tears of anguish and frustration as Mothers and Fathers try gain enough pay bills, for water, for shelter, for food, warmth, taxes and every basic necessity monetised by the elite who throw down their crumbs! The world has enough wealth to ensure no one hungers, no one is without shelter sanitary and clean environments. But the wealth is held by a small few 1% owning 80% of the Worlds wealth! (Oxfam / The Red Cross 2016). The 1% have no concern for the suffering of the many! Concerning themselves only with Psychopathic Self Serving greed and power! Greed for domination of our beautiful Planet and the "useless eaters" (Henry Kissinger) who's function is to serve them while they watch 250,000 people a day die of hunger! It is no coincidence the European Union Unelected Representatives of the 1% feel threatened by Brexit as it slows down their plans for a "New World Order" (George W Bush) my heart and the hearts of many cry out for justice for the Murdered Starved Cold and the Hungry, the Falsely Imprisoned and the Homeless. For the Families who daily slave to ensure their children don't starve sacrificed on the Alter of greed! These are personal conclusions gained after Travel, and intensive study and research of the Geo Political and Financial activities occurring on our Planet. These observations are missed by most, as attention is given to daily survival and the Main Stream Media messages.

CHAPTER 37

Meditation

My first real Meditation came in India. I had chosen to go to India after an experience as a Nurse left me curious. While working as a Staff Nurse in the discharge department of a large General Hospital. I was to collect a man from a Ward on the sixth floor, and bring him down to the Discharge Lounge to sign papers and go home in pre-arranged transport. On arrival at the ward he was sitting in a wheelchair ready to leave. Jim was aged 85yrs, white hair smartly cut, and well dressed. He was slim build with bright sparkling blue eyes. I introduced myself and explained the discharge procedure. He shook my hand saying cheerfully "let's go". On our way out of the ward, Patients and Staff stopped Jim to say "good bye" and to say "thank you"? I wondered why so many were saying "thank you"?

Waiting for the lift to arrive I asked Jim "why so many thanks"? Jim ignored the question and asked me "do you have pain in your lower back"? I had suffered a lower back pain at that time for 10 years from a lifting injury! I had learned to live with the discomfort but there were no visible signs of my pain!? I asked Jim "how he noticed" he replied "just instinct" then asked me "do you want me to fix it"?? Dementia and confusion came to mind, I felt embarrassed and not sure how to deal with the situation without giving offence? "Thank you Jim for asking, what makes you think you can fix my back". Jim explained to me how as a SAS soldier parachuted into Africa with several other troopers. They camped in the dessert dressed as Nomad dessert travellers but at night, they'd sneak out and attack German supplies then return to the dessert.

While there they were befriended by a dessert Tribe and the "Shaman" the Healer and Leader of the tribe had taken a special interest in Jim, teaching Jim meditations and the Shamans way of Healing others. After many months with the Tribe he had knowledge and ability, preparing via Meditation he could Heal others! He practiced Healing successfully after the war until the day of our meeting.

Arriving at the Discharge Lounge pushing Jim in the Wheelchair he put his foot down stopping the Chair asking "do you want me to fix your back? It will take a couple of minutes" My Nurse Colleagues and several Doctors were watching! Feeling self-conscious, but not wanting to offend I said "ok go ahead" turning my back to him" without touching me he raised his hands behind me. I felt a hot heat at the spot of my discomfort. The heat lasted for several minutes then he stated "give it half an hour or so and it will be fine"!? "Right OK Jim" I thanked him wishing him the best and he left with a cheerful "goodbye" Half hour later my back no longer ached!? And I've not suffered since!

CHAPTER 38

Dreams of Travel

So began my dream of going to India, to learn what it was that Jim was able to do, how was it done? This was in 2008. After my Wife and I met, I stated that I had several items on my "to do list" after we became man and Wife. She agreed we would do these things together. I had spent my adult life formulating and achieving goals and wanted to achieve as much as possible. On to do list were 1-Creating a Business 2-Travel to India and Learn Healing 3-Live abroad in a warmer less oppressive Country 4-Write a book. My goals were achievable and in 2008 I had given myself three years to achieve all three! I think my Wife thought it was wishful thinking, but agreed anyway! As I write this book nearing its completion in 2017 all 4 goals have been completed! What's next???

Start a Business we did, while I continued working at the Prison. I also searched successfully for a place to work and live abroad. The business plus earnings from my work gave us four quality holiday breaks abroad a year.

We learned to sail a thirty-foot yacht in the Greek Ionian Sea, gaining our Weekend Skippers Licence. I drove a diamond black convertible sports car, and we owned several properties. After finding work and accommodation abroad we could live and worked, while enjoying warmer weather and a less oppressive political climate. I felt at the time the UK was oppressive with all Government department joined by technology and recession was in full swing. Being in debt to banks, tax payers baling banks out who appeared too big to fail and too big to goal had become the norm. Each person I was meeting in the UK told me their tale of debt and stress. They were living in fear and I swore not to allow myself to live in fear and stress.

After attending the Wedding of my Daughter in Gibraltar, I knew this was the place I wanted us to live. I applied and was offered a post in Gibraltar as a RGN Nurse in 2009 so my second goal had been achieved.

For several years my Wife and I partied like youngsters in the beautiful Mediterranean sunshine. It was wonderful not to be trapped in doors because of poor weather, never to have to watch TV or listen to constant advertisements always interfering with the watching of a good Movie. The evenings became exciting to look forward to. We would walk around the Rock, travel to adjoining Spain Portugal and Morocco, or just sit looking out over the Sea with a cool drink in the warm evenings.

Watching the Sun go down over the horizon, mesmerised by the Suns reflection sparkling like a thousand diamonds on the dark Sea between Africa Spain and Gibraltar. Each Countries lights reflecting the colours that stretched and danced across the Sea, creating an always changing seascape. Large and small sea birds swooping diving screeching loudly at the fishing boats below. Sitting until 10-11pm in the warm evenings, eating a late supper, chatting friends transfixed by the beauty of the scene. It was a wonderful way to end each day after working on a busy Ward! Then we'd wander slowly home content and ready for sleep.

Our modern blue windowed Apartment was on the third floor of 15 with a huge balcony overlooking the Sea. Views of the harbour Casino's Bars and Restaurants all brightly lit with neon lighting. The music of Jazz Rock Classical and Spanish flamenco could be heard in the distance as Sailboats glided in and out of the harbour. Many friends and family joined us for Holidays or short breaks from the UK, and returned home with fun memories of their stay. Lots of real and lovely people became our friends and together we had crazy mad nights in Spain Gibraltar and Africa, drinking was the national pastime and we didn't let our side down.

After several years it was time to settle another item on "to do list" visit India! I had longed to go for a long time. Wanting to learn Meditation, and the Healing ways taught to my healer Jim. We discussed and decided we'd make the trip as soon as possible avoiding all tourist routes! all on a shoestring budget of £4500 for five months away include flights, food and accommodations along the way. To make it more of an adventure we'd also visit Thailand Vietnam and USA California!

We felt exciting like children before our Social Conditioning, before work and debt took our sense of child wonderment away. It felt great giving four weeks' notice to my Employer. Organising Air flights and what not to take was fraught with decisions as we were taking only one Backpack each and space was scarce! I could feel the butterflies in my tum each day for a month before we left! We received the usual warnings from family and friends, telling us "it was unsafe" … "don't trust anyone" … "be careful" we listened out of respect, but nothing was going to stop us having our adventure! Fear is an imaginary monster lurking in dark corners conjured up after being programmed by Parents Schooling Governments Movies and Main Stream Media constantly pumping Fear Porn messages to the masses! I haven't purchased a Newspaper in 20 years, wont watch TV! I believe Mainstream Media are tools to dumb down and control the masses! The controllers being six large Global Corporations! Maybe one day soon, all will be revealed and the meaning of "Conspiracy" will take on a new meaning!

We arrived in India January 2012. It was one of the most exciting and wonderful times of my life. Our Qatar Airliner touched down in Mumbai 8pm after a 16-hour flight from Heathrow Airport! We had travelled for over 30 hours and exhausted by the journey. The Mumbai Airport was modern, air conditioned with a strong resemblance to many other International Airport Terminals, that is, until we got outside!

We got through luggage collection, but on reaching the outskirts of the airport, it was a mass of crazy noisy smelly confusion! Old beat up dusty Taxi cars. Taxi drivers in long colourful gowns, many with turbans on their heads. Calling loudly with waving arms and in broken English "Taxi mam cheap for Taxi". Each on being told our destination, offered many varying Rupee prices, from the ridiculous to the obviously extortionate. I was alive with the energy of all around me, the air was alive with the stink of dung and dust Car horns sounding from near and far. While we were negotiating with one, several other drivers were calling at us not to go with him, go with them! Offering a better price. We eventually decided on a beat up battered old Ford.

The driver tried to get the back door open for us, succeeding only by brute force! Inside the car, stuffing had come out of several large holes in the seating. Stowing our backpacks in the boot, driver got in it was like an oven in the car, the stink and dust from outside made us cover our nose and mouth with linen scarfs so we could breathe easier. We asked the driver to put the window up and turn on the Air conditioning, the driver said "sorry please, no air Condit missy no no no" whilst shaking his head from side to side! The Hotel we had booked for one night was only 3 miles from the airport!!

On the way we tried to wind up the windows again without success. He drove like a mad man, weaving in and out of Bicycles Motor Bikes High loads of Plastic Bottles Cart Horses Cows and People! Horns screeching brakes, shouting voices, barking dogs, and families living on the roadside cooking food over a fire all my senses were on fire! I didn't know where to look first, it was chaotic and I felt alive and exhilarated by it all! The car smelt like stale curry and musky sweat, the heat unbearable, we got a window down by brute force, then quickly closed it again as the hot, tepid smelly air assailed our nostrils! We kept our light scarfs to our faces fascinated by it all. The driver appeared not to have an idea of the highway Code! Horns screeched as other Drivers narrowly missed each other! Woman Children Men and Beast walked in the road! Being narrowly missed by the oncoming Traffic all competing for a way through the chaos. Even at 9pm at night it took an hour to drive 3 miles!

On arrival at our hotel, we paid the driver, who we now noticed had many teeth missing, the remaining Teeth were brown and broken. He pointing to a dark, high gated building. It was pitch black darkness with no lighting! The faecal smells much stronger out of the car, Dogs barked loudly, my Wife was tearful and I reassured her that "we were ok".

In the darkness we searched for an entrance to the Hotel. While searching, a small olive skinned man approached us in the darkness as if from nowhere! "what do you want here" shaking his head from side to side as he spoke. He scared us with his surprise appearance. We explained we had a reservation for one night, and trying to find an entrance to the Hotel. "oh good evening and welcome to our beautiful hotel, please follow me", we followed tired worn and very hot, Back Packs feeling much heavier now than remembered. The Night Guard stopped at high double iron gates, keys jangling releasing a huge Padlock. He pushed the gates open bidding us to follow. With a Torch he lit our way along a path to the entrance, unlocked it stepped in and beckoned us on. I wondered when he would turn on some lighting? Switching on an electric light he pointed to a computer and telephone saying "Passports please" head shaking vigorously side to side!

The décor was of coloured natural wall paintings, depicting scenes of cattle grazing in sparse grassland amidst distant hills. Wall carvings of Indian Gods Lions and Elephants. We were fascinated and the amount of artistry of this small reception area. We gave over our passports, signed the Reception and received Wi-Fi passcode paid with a small fee in advance! We were shown to a sparsely furnished Room with double bed and wardrobe. All was in Pinks Gold Yellows and Reds. We thanked our porter and said "Goodnight" he hesitated wanting a tip, but I was in no mood to hunt through my backpack

Diamond in the Stone

for cash, we were both exhausted! We fell onto the bed staring up at the Tobacco stained ceiling. It was pitch black outside with no street lighting, even with the windows closed the rancid smell was prevalent. After minutes in silence hot and sweaty. Several Dogs continually barked as if in reply to each other, then another and another! The wailing howling and barking kept us in semi wakefulness all night. The Dogs finally stopped barking around dawn, then we slept until 13.00 hrs in a deep peaceful sleep.

It was the beginning of our journey, I wanted to find those who taught and practiced Jims art of Healing. The Internet allowed me to locate a very experienced Master Teacher in Kerala on the midwest coast of India, but I had agreed first to spend some time at the Golden Temple to learn Meditation in the mountains of Girah Creek Mumbai, were we had booked a ten-days. Here I was to learn Equanimity, the goal being Higher Consciousness.

We had planned the journey well, stopping at predetermined locations to experience Indian Culture as much as possible. We didn't want Tourist Hotels only traditional that were clean. We awoke feeling dirty and hot, with the intention to travel by Bus and Ferry Boat to Fort Kochi. My wife informed me she had cried a lot during the night, saying "she hated the filth and smells of human faeces, noise and this dirty Hotel room"! The Sunny blue skies made us both feel better as we made our way in turn to Shower. The Cockroaches had gotten there before us! My Wife's screams of "Mummy Mummy" from the Bathroom Shower Cubicle alerted me to several large black Beetles an inch long with pincers on their heads! Unclothed and half asleep, I caught and wrapped each in Toilet Paper throwing them out of the room window. The Shower water was tepid, slightly yellow but cooling, washing the dust and sweat away, we felt ready for the journey ahead. We changed our English clothing for Indian Sari and Jalapa, tea shirts and cotton scarfs which were very comfortable. We repacked our Backpacks were ready for breakfast. We only had a vague clue in what direction to go from the Hotel. We had a Map and asking direction from the local People would get us to where we wanted to go!

We had missed breakfast we were told after carrying our Backpacks down thread bear stair carpet! The Reception looked nicer in the midday Sun streaming through large windows, with views of climbing plants and shrubs lining the path to the entrance gate. The smell was wafting in through the open windows, but not over powering as the day before. "There was a small café upstairs" the Porter from the night before told us head shaking side to side. I wondered where he had slept, then noticed a sleeping roll behind the desk! He was the Proprietor Cleaner Gardener Cook and slept behind the desk!!

We decided to eat and drink first, before stressing over directions. The Café was several tables in a small room windows opening to a wonderful view of the dusty streets of India. Breakfast was a very tasty Masala Dosa with a curry spiced creamy liquid which we spread on cheesy tortillas and a cup of milky sweet Chai Tea.

Afterwards, Backpacks on our backs, we stepped out into the blazing hot dusty street, grey dust covered everything, the stink assailed our nostrils again. Broken street curbing, tired looking corrugated roofed brick houses with pieces of rag or cardboard for curtains. Human waste lay in places covered in black flies, some landing on our faces arms and legs, any body part that was not covered. We were dumb struck, my wife was disgusted, holding her nose, I thought she was going to throw up. Olive skinned people looked at us with curious looks as we tried to hurry across the dust covered Road which was a big mistake!

To get to the other side of the Road, we dodged Cars Bikes Wooden Carriages Bicycles Trucks, and emaciated Donkeys with packs on their backs, looking like they may collapse at any moment! My wife was screaming "Mommy Mommy" in fear of being knocked down. While still trying to swat the flies away, I took her arm reassuring and pulled her forward. At one point she froze in the middle of the chaotic traffic, shouting "I don't like this" I was thinking "this is amazing" it felt like I was alive for the first time in my whole life! We were trying to get to the Ferry that would take us across the River to Fort Kochi. Several friendly locals told us "a Bus would take us to a town close to the Jetty" We had booked a Bed and Breakfast accommodation using the internet to book our room at Fort Kochi. Getting to the Jetty by Bus was an adventure.

The heat and chaos were our biggest hurdles. Families had built makeshift homes out of cardboard polythene with corrugated rusting tin roofs. Small children played together in groups kicking pop cans and plastic bottles. The children appeared healthy smiling laughing and oblivious to the chaos and poverty around them. The Shops where makeshift affairs, looking like poorly made garden sheds with open fronts. Some of the men appeared to be working, taking engines, metal bits and pieces apart and paid us no attention.

Beggar children hands outstretched crying "dollar mister, dollar missy" we gave small amounts to a few, quickly realising that we could end up giving all our money away, so stopped giving. We waited at the curb side for the bus to arrive, when it did, it was a battered 40 seat rusting heap, with no glass in any of the windows! It was crowded with cotton wrapped woman, men and children surrounded by old bags, boxes, suitcases and assorted bundles. We paid several Rupees to a smiling non English speaking driver, who eventually gave us a ticket. The people on the Bus stared vacantly at us, seats were hard held together by rusting chrome covered tubing. I got on the Bus wearing a white cotton shirt, after travelling for two hours, the shirt was dusty brown! Our hands legs feet and faces were covered in dust. We had loaded more than several 2 litre plastic bottles of water into our Backpacks which we drunk quickly to avoid dehydration. The small shops sold chilled water and we became a regular Customers in our Months in India.

The Ferry Jetty area was a hot mass of heaving humanity young and old, a hot sweaty snake of people inching forwards to a large flat wooden Boat. It had three decks crammed with people, large bundles and luggage. When I say "large bundles" I mean the size of dog kennels! Some actually carrying these bundles on their heads! After an eternity of queuing, we got on the Ferry shoving and dragging the backpacks (which now felt like ton weights) up the ramp onto the overcrowded Ferry.

We both let out a large sigh of relief! Getting from the Hotel to here had been like trekking through a dense overgrown jungle, but more crowded! We remained standing the whole way across that River, squashed on all sides by travellers. The boat roof and wind cooled and our sweaty hot bodies. It was heaven in comparison to the smelly traffic, crowded streets and roads. Seeing "Fort Kochi" in the distance we wondered "would it be more of the same"? I don't think we could have survived another day like the last 24 hours!

The Ferry at last arrived at the Jetty in Fort Kochi about 2.30pm. My first impression was of a much calmer place and the smell gone! To my relief no major roadways, just small streets and Shop stalls. Our first objective was to find our accommodation, a shower change clothing, stow our packs away and get something to eat before exploring the Island. We obtained a Map from an information Kiosk not far from the Jetty, we were not far from our Accommodation.

Streets were worn natural surfaces carved over long periods by pedestrians and traffic. A lot of the brick constructed buildings we noted along the small streets appeared British in their architecture, with fabulous and intricately carved solid wooden doors, dating back at least a hundred years or more and very attractive. Every one we stopped for directions spoke good English and welcomed us to their island. It was hot but the breeze from the river made it pleasant, the weariness of the Mumbai began to dissolve. Street stalls made of tarpaulin wood and plastic, displayed hand written signs encouraging visitors to their stalls. Selling everything from food, fresh fish, drinks, clothing, electrical home appliances, hippy paraphernalia and fruit. Stall sellers called to us as we walked by. We purchased fresh orange juice and water, enjoying sipping our drinks while sitting on a wooden bench in a grassed area. The local fishermen were drawing Chinese nets attached to catapult like wooden structures fixed to the shoreline, lifting up and lowering down to the River, only small numbers of crabs and fish were being netted? But they continued up and down, up and down, it was peaceful and beautiful. We forced ourselves to get up and search for our Accommodation and surprised to find a Cricket field, Park and trees and beautiful wood and stone buildings with a British twist! We found the Accommodation but disappointed when we were told the price had gone up overnight!? Thinking we were being scammed we found another place not far away! Amazing and cheap too. An English style BB managed by friendly local Asian Indians, designed of stone, carved varnished wooden beams, ornately colourful. Everything was immaculately clean, and facing the Cricket Pitch.

We loved it on sight booking it for a week! The bedroom was very clean and we settled in quickly, we showered changed and couldn't wait to get back out and explore our new surroundings. We were not disappointed, everywhere we walked we found traces of the English colonisation of India, which had left a unique blend of everything from food to Architecture and landscape. Best of all was the people themselves, humble helpful peaceful with a smile and a welcome.

It is a shame that they like we, sometimes found life difficult and extreme, for the lack of money. People deserve better, "those who control the money control the people and the world" as a member of the Rothschild family once said!

Visiting other countries, experiencing different cultures, I've become aware of the differences, Political and Social, but we have a great deal in common i.e. we laugh cry mourn feel pain, love and want to be loved, all want to be happy. The biggest common denominator is "Money"! Wealth is so disproportionately distributed; we get what we are able to earn or borrow from the Banks. So few hold vast wealth while others starve, have no home, no educational opportunities, clean water or Health Care? Why do so few own the wealth? In the West we at have opportunities through Education or Wealth. Somewhere inside of me, I know this is not the way it should be!

Character Assassination

A strange threatening event occurred 1 month into our India trip. I received a phone call from my Nurse Registration body NMC. They had been contacted by an anonymous source in Gibraltar, who notified them of my Teenage Criminal Record and questioned why I was a Nurse! I couldn't believe my ears. I gave my professional body NMC a full written report of my juvenile history. They agreed to get back to me after a meeting to review my registration. I was shocked that after so many years and great effort in all areas of my life, that I may regarded as a criminal! It took several weeks for them to get back to me, my registered Nurse RGN licence to practice would remain! I discovered later that a person who I had worked with in Gibraltar and disgruntled I had been Nominated for a Nurse of the Year Award. They then gained unauthorised access to my work records and set out to discredit me. After my break travelling.

I returned to Gibraltar to put a formal complaint to the Minister for Health and Chief Minister, but I got nowhere! It appeared many on that Rock were related and the complaint door was well and truly shut! The disclosure of another person's personal information is an offence punishable by law covered by the Data Protection Act. The offence was covered up to protect those involved. I have never withheld my teenage past from any of my employers, and did not appreciate this attack on my character. The Rehabilitation of Offenders Act 1975 is supposed to protect past juvenile offenders!

As a professional Nurse I have to disclose all offences, even "spent convictions" as I work with vulnerable people. But it concerns me that no individual assessment is made so as to allow expungement of juvenile criminal history, of a person who has evidenced total rehabilitation. The 1975 Act does not protect an Individual from bias and or persons wishing to Character assassinate? In these circumstances the ex-Offenders should be considered as vulnerable! This was not to be the last time, but any question of my character were dismissed! My heart knows me, my love and respect for myself is my strength in such times, however it did shake up world!

CHAPTER 39

Meditation in India "it will pass"

We arrived at the Golden Pagoda in Gorai Creek Mumbai travelling from 6am for 6 hours by crowded Trains Ferry Boat and finally horse and cart! The horse collapsed at one point, hoofs slipping on hard rocky dust covered track. The driver used his whip to get the horse to stand back up, my wife cried for the horse's exhaustion and demanded "please let the Horse rest and drink" which he did and the Horse recovered after a twenty-minute respite and water, which we purchased for the Horse from a ramshackle hut Shop!

The Shop was dark with a crowd of bright eyed smiling children outside, looking at us like we were Hollywood Stars! We gave the children a few Rupees then rode the rest of the way in silence admiring the views, hanging on for dear life! It was late afternoon when we arrived at the Temple. The Sun was blazing hot, we were dirty tired and filled with apprehension. Was it going to be a bunch of new age hippies chanting Hara Krishna? Part of me begrudged being tied down for 10 days, I wanted to spend the whole time exploring beautiful India. My wife had done a 10-day Silent Meditation in England so knew what to expect, but not me!

The Temple was a large golden topped Monastery some parts still under construction. I was told Buddha's Ashes were held here, making it for me, even more special! There were no People outside, only the occasional work man and several huge rats scurried about. The scenery was spectacular overlooking Mountains and green hills. A sign pointed us to a reception area. At reception we were directed by white robed very calm assistants, who welcomed us, and requested that we fill out required information and leave our Passports with the clerk.

I changed clothing for white cotton top and loose cotton trousers. Stowed our belongings in an allotted numbered locker, no Books Mobile Phones Cigarettes or un essential personal items were to be taken into the Meditation area. Females went through one door, Males through another door to allocated accommodation. Silence was to be strictly maintained for 10 days from now, quiet communication could take place with the Teachers only and nobody else! I said goodbye to my Wife which didn't make me feel comfortable at all! I felt like I was going into Prison and having all my rights taken away! What was I doing? I should be enjoying my exploration of India! Accommodation was a single whitewashed room resembling a Prison Cell!

A wood constructed bed, a thin rolled up cushion mattress, several sheets and a blanket, with a wash basin small toilet and shower. One small meshed covered window and nothing else! I was beginning to feel very claustrophobic apprehensive and wanted to get out of there! But I was alone, Passport taken and all doors to the Reception had been locked after arriving to my Cell area! Right, I thought "you're here, give it a chance and see how it turns out"! I showered, changed into my white cotton clothing.

A tinkling bell sounded, a knock came at my door, I opened it, a white gowned shaved headed assistant informed me politely "it was tea time". He directed me to a large Hall. Here, about 60 People milled about Males and Females, all ages. Some appeared comfortable and smiling, others, like me appeared nervous, eyes darting here and there, looking for escape! Apprehension written on their faces. It seemed to me these People were also asking "what the hell am I doing here"? I was definitely feeling outside of my comfort zone! Funnily enough, the words "I'm a Celebrity, get me out of here" came to mind. We were told by the assistant that after we leave this Hall, we were not allowed to speak anymore accept to Teachers or by requesting quietly of one of the assistants, who would relay our queries to a Teacher. We received a Video presentation about Meditation after we had eaten and drank sufficient.

At 8pm we would Meditate for an hour then bed time until first day Meditation began at 4am! I was thinking "what! Get up at 4am to meditate! This is crazy"! The food was Vegan with lots of raw and cooked Vegetables Curries Rice Pastas Fresh Fruits Warm Chai Tea Natural Herbal drinks and Water. I relaxed a little and sought out friendly looking others, and made small talk about our journeys here, knowing afterwards I would not get another opportunity to speak for 10 days! The Video was interesting, outlining the 10-day program which would be hard!

We were told "the mind would resist and be tormented by being ignored, but we would learn to be Equanimeous if we persevered, we would learn the breathing techniques of Meditation eventually all difficulties would pass". The Video presentation lasted an hour, then made our way to a large spacious Meditation Hall. Females one side Males the other! We all sat on the floor in rows of 8 at both sides of the Hall. In front of the Hall was a raised platform with a cushioned seat, for the bald headed, white gowned Teacher who sat crossed legged in quiet Meditation. Behind to the right of the Teacher was a White Projector Screen, the Hall was in semi darkness.

When we had selected cushions and blankets, trying to make my crossed legs comfortable, I constantly changed the position, propping them up with smaller cushions. Eventually after a good 10 minutes all settled and the screen came to life. Mr Goenka small and stout, round dark face smiled out at us, and instructed us on how we should breath, settle our minds and be still for the next hour! The screen then returned to blank and I followed his instruction to the letter, but my mind would not shut up! Yap Chatter Chatter "concentrate dammit" I told myself! Trying to keep my awareness my breath in breath out. I occasionally became aware of the warm breath leaving my nostrils and the cold breath entering.

Feeling every movement of the breath, my awareness became more focussed after 15 minutes, but thoughts pushed to the surface demanding attention. The battle between my awareness on breathing and thought interruptions continued for the next hour! My back and knees cried out for relief. At the end of an hour, a light tinkling bell indicated the end of the session. I nearly fell backwards with relief! My legs, knees and bottom had frozen painfully locked into position. The pain of uncrossing them was almost unbearable, it took me awhile to get off the floor!

I made my way, tired and stiffly to my Cell in silence, nobody else saying a word either. Stripping off my clothing quickly, I crashed onto the bed and into a deep exhausted peaceful sleep. A soft bell ringing and a knock at my door told my sleeping mind it was 4am! Time to get up for a meditation session, it was dark and silent, and here I was getting up to practice Meditation! I was told at the presentation, the 4am Meditation could be carried out in the bedroom, I knew if I did that, I would fall asleep. Sleepily, I washed dressed and made my way to the Hall. The Hall was in semi darkness and about seventy people sat crossed legged in silence. The Teacher on his gold seat, crossed legged looking serene and peaceful. It took forever to quietly gather to me cushions, blanket and several little foam blocks to support my back, knees and legs. Getting comfortable was almost impossible.

Eventually I settled, with a straight back, hands resting on my already aching knee joints. Silence and sleepy peaceful feelings began to descend onto my mind, I was falling back into sleep, "no" I screamed at my mind "you are not going to sleep" I sent awareness to the tepid cool movement of my inhaled breath and the warm outbreath as it left my lungs, then gently flowing out of both nostrils. Behind my eyelids I could see only darkness. I began to feel very peaceful, no thoughts, no mind chatter, no bodily discomforts! Just then the loudest snoring sound exploded in my ears from the Asian chap sitting crossed legged two feet to my right! My peace was shattered, like a train had just pulled into the station with screeching brakes. My peace was gone! "Come back" I begged myself, but it was too late!

I began to hear Coughs Sniffing Fidgeting every sound and movement felt and heard by my awakened awareness! I felt a panic running through me "Peace Please come back" my mind screamed. I knew from our presentation the night before; I must become one with my breathing! So, ignoring my mind chatter which I now considered a naughty chattering monkey, always seeking my attention. Ignoring the Monkeys, I again focused awareness on breath in- breath out- breath in- breath out! The Monkey shook its cage and jumped about with constant chatter demanded my attention!

But awareness remained on my breath which was cool and soothing. Breathe out like warm soft silk leaving my nasal passages with gentle almost inaudible sound, the warmth caressing my top lip entering into silent peace. The sounds were still around me, but I allowed all sounds to pass by, not giving them any attention! Breath in- breath out. It was amazing! I was actually Meditating in complete silence! The Monkey mind chatter got less and I floated in peaceful silence. Behind my eyelids I began to see various colours, florescent soothingly and soft. I wanted to stay in this peace forever, a metallic tinkling Bell brought me back to earth, session had ended! The pain in my back and knees returned. I had been Meditating for two hours, were the heck did it go? On reflection, I now knew what the Teacher meant when he said "my mind would fight back and resist attempts to ignore it" This was my first real battle and I had succeeded! It was now 6am. We could have a break in silence, to sit on one of many Benches, or walk around the Garden before Meditation at 7 am back in the hall. I chose to walk around the soft gravel flowered and hedged Garden.

While walking in silence, I tried to retrace the steps of my first real Meditation. Strangely, my mind did not want to wake up! I imagined it was having a tantrum saying "I'm not speaking to you, you ignored me, I'm ignoring you"! Instead of thoughts and mind chatter, I was feeling sensations, the soft gravel beneath my sandaled feet, cool air brushing my body, warmth from the rising Sun. I heard the Insects as they flew and crawled. Wow! I felt the soft cotton shirt against my skin, sounds of bird song, and thought I felt the flapping whooshing of air beneath their wings and my body! Something was changing and it felt great! I was fascinated alert and alive!

7 am arrival, returning to the Hall, I the usual 5-10-minute settle down period, as I tried to prepare my space and make myself comfortable. My Monkey chatter began "it's going to be uncomfortable, go back to bed, it will hurt my knees" etc. I eventually settled down Eyes closed Legs crossed, my Back and Neck straight. I took 3 slow deliberate deep breaths, letting the Monkey chatter pass.

My awareness on the sensations of cool breath in, warm breath out. My breathing settled to a slow gentle movement. Occasionally Monkey brought a memory or circumstance to mind demanding response and answers! Breathe in - breathe out letting Monkey speak to himself! I began floating gently into that peaceful place, warm sensations of breath. Behind my eyelids colours floated gently by like clouds on a sunny day, it was beautiful!

The tinkling metal bell sounded, signalling it was time to come back. I resisted allowing myself to remain breathing peacefully. The noises from the People leaving the Hall brought me back. Opening my eyes still in a trancelike state, I urged myself to rise, it was a conscious effort of will, I didn't want to return!

8am breakfast time. The Canteen filled with silent bodies moving quietly and ghost like! Inspecting and choosing from colourful rows of fruit, warm porridge, breads, yogurts, natural cereals, many cold and hot drinks, nobody spoke! The instruction on arrival was to "avoid eye contact with any, but the Teacher". "Surreal" is an understatement, we were all in a semi-conscious state, like zombies! Speaking for myself, my mind was totally at ease, my movements slow and deliberate, feeling all bodily sensations.

Feet Hands and Arms all felt slightly out of sync with my mind! I carried my selection to a benched seating area. My mouth was alive! Every morsel, every movement of the tongue and swallowing appeared slowed down! My sensations of taste sharpened. I looked around without making eye contact "were they feeling the way I was feeling"? It was truly fascinating! A totally different way of experiencing the world!

After breakfast we again chose how we would spend our silent break time until 10 am when we would return to the Hall. Walking with a still mind all my senses alive, my sight hearing, touch and smell magnified each experience, in what I can only describe as "aliveness". Again returning to the Hall, getting comfortable adjusting my position, legs crossed back and neck straight, blanket around shoulders, hands resting on my knees and eyes closed. I took my first deep gentle inhalation, feeling every movement of the air as it entered my body, the peace immediately caressed me then "Boom" it began. Explosive noises of hydraulic drill hammers, shovels grating on hard ground, squeaky wheel barrows, booted feet walking to and fro! My peace was shattered! What the… was going on? I heard the fidgeting of people in the hall. I tried to ignore the sounds sending my awareness back to my breath. For short periods I achieved peace, but for the next two hours it was a battle! The Monkeys were on the side of the builders and the noises outside!

CHAPTER 40

"It will Pass"

It was 12 noon, the building noises and my battle had gone on for two hours until lunch time. The bell called a halt to my struggle. I thought "this can't be right, I come here to Meditate and a building site appears" the silence had gone! I needed to talk to the Teacher, who was still sitting crossed legged, serene like nothing had changed! The teacher was always the last to leave, he remained in the Hall to answer questions after Meditation was over. We were expected to walk silently to the front of the hall, kneel in front of him if we had a question. His seat was on a raised platform 2 feet above the hall. I waited kneeling head slightly bowed and waited for his attention, he looked at me and asked "What can I do for you my son?" I asked him politely looking up "You know I came here to learn to Meditate" he replied "yes my son how can I assist you?" I asked "how can I meditate when there are sounds of Pneumatic drills and building site activity?" calmly he told me "My son, it will pass" I understood him to mean that the building works would cease, all would be well. I felt reassured, I bowed chin to chest, hands together in prayer, saying "thank you" he bowed back with a faint smile, his eyes closed signalling my dismissal, so off I went to lunch at the Canteen. After a two-hour lunch break in the garden trying to calm my Monkey, which wouldn't let go of the building site situation, which by the way, I could still hear! I returned to the Hall. All was well, until the workmen

Diamond in the Stone

began again pounding, shovelling and scraping, omg my Monkey was going crazy! Two hours I fought to focus on my breath, bang squeak thump scrape! I found peace for several short periods when the drilling stopped, then it started again, my Monkey had not shut up for two hours! I was definitely going to see Teacher again! The tinkling bell sounded, I was up and at the front in a gif! Teacher "yes my son how can I assist you?" looking him in the eyes I stated "you said it would pass, it's still very loud! What's going on?" looking down with a smile "my son it will pass" he was starting to really irritate me and my Monkey! "You said that before, but it's still here"! Smiling he asked "would you like to go to a Cell to meditate?" what! A Cell, what was going on! "What do you mean a Cell?" he smiled "I will have an assistant take you to a quiet Cell around the back" I couldn't believe my ears "a Cell" round the back! He rang the brass bell and a bald headed white cotton gowned assistant arrived almost immediately, and instructed to take me to the Cells round the back!

The "Cells" around the back were rows of what looked like steel Telephone boxes but sound proofed! Like a Dr Who Tardis's side by side and numbered. Inside the Cell there was a cushion on the floor and the steel door had a movable disc covered Spyhole! "What the…." I couldn't believe my eyes and ears! The assistant asked me to "enter No 32 Cell" instructing me to "press the Red Button on the wall if I required help!" I asked if "he was joking?" I stated "the sun is already baking me"! he smiled "another button on the wall will allow airflow whilst inside" I asked him to "take me back to the Hall" he left me at the Canteen as it was now tea time. After 6pm the builders all went home, thank goodness! Peace returned and Meditating from 6pm to 9pm was a joy! I approached the Teacher each day for three days, hands in prayer, asking "when will the building noise pass?" receiving the smiling reply "it will pass my son" I discovered at the end of the third day they were building more Cells and would finish in a week! That was it, I couldn't take the noise any longer! After breakfast on the fourth day I had decided I was leaving! I approached the Teacher kneeling, hands in prayer and smilingly he asked "yes my son how can I assist you?"

I'd had enough of his "it will pass" I said "please return my Passport, I'm leaving and I mean now!" he was taken aback "but my son it will pass" I repeated "please get my Passport now"! I stood saying "I will be at the Reception area and expect Clothes Property and Passport returned to me"! he stood up paying attention for the first time in four days, the smile had gone "you will have to speak to the Senior Teacher, please wait I will get him" An hour passed before the Senior Teacher arrived! He asked me into his office saying "take a seat" then asked "what is the problem my Son?" I explained the noise and building work and stated "I would like my Passport Property and Clothing returned, I'm leaving!" He said irritating me "but it will pass my Son"! Leaning forward, ignoring his remark, I repeated "please get my Passport now! Please!" He asked "what about your Wife?" I requested he let her know I was leaving, and if she wanted to stay "I would meet her in Goa on the West Coast of India"! After more fuss and attempts to get me to stay, we received our Passports and Property and left!

But something had changed! I had discovered that my Monkey mind had controlled me all my life! But I now knew I was supposed to control it! Real me was not my mind! My true self was in the Awareness of the Now and Connected to All! I now knew what it meant in the Bible to "Peace be still" and "seek ye first the kingdom of Heaven and all things will be added unto thee" that "the kingdom of Heaven is within" it all made sense now, and was a lesson never to be forgotten! Later that year I completed a 10-day silent Meditation in Hereford UK.

Meditating daily has become my greatest pleasure, "wealth has not given me peace as the minute I got it I started worrying about losing it or making more. Peace is now my greatest treasure"! On beginning my Meditation now, random thoughts still appear, but tip toe quietly away as awareness goes to breath. My mind remains quiet outside and inside of Meditation free of fears! Being aware of the Now, Peacefulness becomes a constant companion. In Meditation my body stills the Mind ceases chatter and Respiratory rate reduces to

7-10 per minute. Heart rate 30 beats per minute! (as recorded during Meditation).

During Meditation my body slightly vibrates spreading from Toes to the top of my Head! These sensations led me to research the experiences of other Meditators. There were those who practised "Chakra" Meditation, and that the body has 7 energy vortexes located along the spine, which can influence the Endocrine System in a very positive way. (1) Base Chakra (2) Pelvic Chakra (3) Solar Plexus Chakra (3) Heart Chakra (4) Throat Chakra (5) Brow Chakra and (6) Crown Chakra. Each responds Intent Specific Colour and Vibrational Tone. It probably sounds a bit mumbo jumbo, it did to me at the time! But I decided to put it to the test.

So, sitting still, allowing all thoughts to pass without giving them notice, beginning with three deep conscious breaths. Filling each breathe with love and exhaling all concerns. I sent my awareness to each Chakra area in turn imagining the corresponding Colour. To my astonishment, I felt sensations warmth and gentle pressure around that Chakra! Beautiful sensations! My health and sense of wellbeing have improved a hundred fold! After several years of daily practice, and behind my Brow Chakra, I see Images of the most astonishing beauty. I see on occasion, images of unknown people? I have experienced my physical location change to another scene elsewhere! Like my spirit has left, and is visiting other places, and always with the most astonishing clarity and colour!

Meditation has affected my waking vision also, as at times I see glistening pinpoints of light appear in the air! Sparkling orbs with metallic yellow white and electric blue. The lights come together into patterns of Geometry! Moving up and down, floating gently in all directions. My clarity at these moments is sharply focused, emotions are of peaceful acceptance of the moment! Beauty of Nature and Life on occasions brings a sense of joy, as I stare in wonder at the mystery of it all!

A friend once said "you have lived like a Cat with nine lives!" My life has been real, filled with Adventures, Challenges Happiness Sadness Love and wonderful people, some harder to love than others. Many years of searching has brought me to this moment. Peace and a sense of wonder and one with all, has come only after hard won internal battles. I have an acceptance of all individuals and feel connected to all beings and things living, which is everything! Importantly, I have a love and respect for myself. And yet, even with this heart felt connection, Ego can surface on occasion.

Spiritual vigilance and self-awareness is an absolute requirement to attain the Peace promised by Jesus when he said "my Peace I give you, but not as the world giveth" Being aware of thoughts arising and sending them away with compassion if they are not for the highest good! "Every breath is a gift of love from above. Inhale this love and exhale it back into the world." We have, I believe been conditioned to judge, condemn and see others as being unworthy. Each of us are worthy, each soul is on their own journey of discovery. "Desire nothing and be content with everything" Often circumstances will determine the choices we will make and John Lennon once sang "whatever gets you through the night" he knew, as I now do, circumstances often dictate our choices. I have lived on the Streets, spent time behind Cell doors, survived threatening circumstances, my choices led me to dark corners where survival was the only objective!

These "dark corners" only the Homeless, the Prisoner, rejected and unloved know! My story of choices has been a Life Worth Living. I have been taken care of by Angels in my darkest loneliest times. They had compassion and hearts that cared for another soul. These Angels too were making their way through a difficult dangerous world! Unity Consciousness is our birth right, and can be attained via humility, compassion and Meditation. We wear masks, but inside we scream to be loved, to be noticed, to be valued, we feel like strangers in this World!

Our negative perceptions, fears and divisions, have been perpetuated by a controlling elite! These are the war makers with an agenda to strengthen their control of Global Wealth and Power. Many sit glued to the TV allowing the control to continue, without knowledge of control the masses are conditioned daily!

At this time, I have maybe 15-20 years yet to live on Earth. What will those years' reveal? Getting old in a society dominated by corporate marketing campaigns, broadcasting through ever expanding technological advanced media, screaming out, be young, be beautiful, be rich. This will relegate the poor, and all who do not fit the money making messages, to be of no value! This is the world I find myself in at this time. So a challenge it will continue to be without doubt. I will remain a loving being. I will see wonderful changes in Global Societies Technologies and Human Empowerment. Wealth will be returned back to its legitimate owners i.e. every soul of the earth!

Mankind's consciousness will shift from I Me and Mine to We Us and Unity Consciousness. And wonderful experiences for all human kind. This New World will begin after those who have perpetuated the enslavement of Mankind, are identified and brought to justice! Their crimes will be of such horrendous magnitude, that humans will experience shock, as the details of those crimes emerge. Service to Others will become the foundations of Governments. The hidden and stolen wealth of the people will be found and redistributed bringing about change on an amazing scale. A Debt Jubilee of Global proportion will celebrate our release from the Criminal Global Corrupt.

Each individual soul will pursue their highest potential in an attitude of Peace Serenity and Joy. They will watch themselves, their children and families thrive. Free of oppression and enslavement, Poverty will cease and architectural structures will once again reflect beauty and geometrical magnificence. Love will become the deciding factor of all things. Peace will reign in all hearts. As a reflection in a mirror, all outward will become a reflection of the inward.

Namaste to all my Brothers and Sisters on and off this world, the harsh realities of enslavement will be no more, ensuring for us all, a peaceful journey into a heaven sent, loving future.

CHAPTER 41

Life's Lessons Hard Won

By radiating cheerfulness and expressing positivity, all beings and living creatures in my immediate surroundings are uplifted.

Giving my complete attention to the individual I am interacting with, gives that individual a gift, the gift of their uniqueness and value.

The verbal opinions of another is their gift of expression to me, a gift to be accepted with grace.

Being conscious of each unfolding moment, is unspoken acceptance and gratitude for all that is.

I am not my thoughts which are only preconditioned egotistical responses given from Parents Society and Schooling.

I do not allow my mind to tell me! I give my mind my commands and it obeys.

I exist right now, not in the past, not in the future. Now is and always will be. Experience life now!!

Allowing dialogue with negative thoughts attracts physical, emotional and mental stress. At these times, awareness brings me back to the beautiful now.

Seeking revenge for perceived hurt from another brings suffering and emotional pain to myself.

Fear is a liar, a thief, which if allowed steals my dreams and my peace.

Fear can be sent lovingly away. When I send it away, fear realisers it is an unwelcome guest and stops calling, my peace returns and dreams unfold.

Awareness that I am connected to all other living beings nurtures my respect for all.

I am an atom in a sea of atoms all intricately connected. When I send love from my heart, it is sent and received.

Acceptance without resistance to my now, allows me to see and be aware of its miracle.

Animals and all living creatures have minds and hearts.

The mind of a child is pure and filled with wonder. Seeking to become childlike is a worthy pursuit.

Nothing is impossible if I believe.

Loving myself was hard won. But has enabled me to love and respect all others. I believe I am they and they are me.

When I hurt another, I hurt myself.

Diligently believing visualising my dreams, has made all my dreams come true without exception.

Holding back an unkind word allows kind words to surface.

Only my mind can stop my happiness and joyful emotions. Control Your Emotions. Reversing a downward spiral takes a bit of effort, and a little time. But you can do it! The effort you put into controlling emotions will give you a sunnier outlook on life and teach you that you have a choice to feel good or not.

I can see so much more when I look within.

Being attached to thoughts, emotions and pains of the past can shut out my now. My loving sincere Forgiveness is required for Peace and Happiness and predicated by Universal law.

Would you stand in front of someone while they were delivering a whole heap of unhealthy, insane, abusive, damaging and disgusting versions of you and your life and listen to it? Understand if you stand there and argue with an abusive individual, you get damaged. If you do this, you have serious problems with setting boundaries. Know that your ego is every bit as abusive as another damaging individual. If

River Blue

you have a 'fight with yourself' you're trying to justify yourself to your ego and convince it you aren't this person, you don't have these fears, you don't have doubts and you really are capable. Your ego loves this because it will trick you into thinking that you can win the argument, that you can convince it and resolve the issue, and that you'll receive peace after having this struggle with yourself. This is so untrue!

Your ego will keep coming back at you again and again, and just like any abusive person who simply won't get it, wants to project fears and doubts, and not find peace within. The argument will continue to resurface and never be healed. Think about this - how exhausting is it trying to argue and justify yourself with a person who is continually abusing you? If you don't disconnect and get away from them, you eventually give in and start agreeing with their version of you just to get some peace. Inevitably if you keep hooking into your ego you'll end up doing the same thing. Eventually you'll be so worn down that you'll accept and agree with the inner dialogue of 'I'm worthless and a failure'.(Melanie Tonia Evans)

Expectations of another are chains of my mind. I am free when I press delete and empty myself of such. Resistance is the battling ego, insisting on having its way.

I love my past; it has given me my present which is my gift.

I understand that the purpose of my life has been to learn that love is the ultimate prize. Love is my wealth and power.

Asking for help requires humility, receiving that help requires my sincere gratitude.

My experiences have given me the opportunity to learn. I have stumbled and fallen occasionally, I've gotten back up, applied what I learned and moved on.

Making love, being one with the one I love, with my whole mind, body and soul, brings us both into a heavenly loving place.

My life has been more meaningful when I have others to enjoy it with.

Diamond in the Stone

Ability and strength have been given to me by my connection to a higher power. I don't know what it is? I do know it is!

I see coloured particles all around me, which comfort me, energise and fill me with wonder. I don't know what they are? I know they are!!

When we Meditate, we see the mind for what it is- sometimes our friend, but usually it limits us. When we can go beyond the mind through the practice of Meditation, we understand we can do anything we wish- if we truly believe we can. We can change the world with our thoughts, we can become psychic, more intuitive, become healers-our mind becomes multidimensional, so we manifest more of that!

The more you are able to identify and put the demanding mind to rest, the awareness of the heart is able to come into play, and the more you acknowledge it and nurture it, the more it will stay with you. (www in 5d)

In meditation I travel to heavenly places, visits from strangers, have visions of future, glide over far away countries and oceans, ascend to far away galaxies and planets. I don't know how? But I do!!

Without Medications my body has healed itself. Don't know how? But it does!

Service to others with compassion has unfolded my true being, and has connected me to a deep happiness.

I know all TV News channels broadcast only what the 6 Corporations allow. Wars past and present, and the deaths of innocent millions have been the result of such criminal manipulation. Justice has been a long time coming, but come it will! When all People's eyes are opened! Collective Consciousness will demand justice.

"Not too long ago, people believed the Earth was flat. They knew it to be true with all their hearts. But then people started sailing all the way around the world and flying from here to there, and we gradually got used to thinking of the earth as globular. We just got used to it. Well, in the same way, it will one day be a matter of common sense to most people that we're all one with the universe. It'll be so simple. And maybe when that happens, we'll handle our technology with better sense. Maybe we'll act with love toward our environment, instead of destroying it. Holiness doesn't mean being good; good people aren't necessarily holy. "A holy person is someone who is whole" Allan Watts

Letter to Myself

Hey, lots of years have gone by, trials and challenges have come your way, and you bravely faced each with courage, and you are still alive!! You turned your life around. You realised you are not your mind! That thoughts and Emotions are manifestations of conditioning, and buried emotional pain. With Courage and Determination, you learned new ways of facing the world. Each day I have watched you strive with a passion to rise above the darkness that has sometimes threatened to sink you into despair, but you never let it! Replacing all negative emotions with Self-Love and Unconditional Love for all. Knowing that the journey of life had to be completed! Sincere Compassion and Love has been your unfailing goal of every new day.

I did notice however; it took longer to realise love for yourself! But then realised, loving yourself is as important as loving others unconditionally! You got it in the end and I'm proud of you! Without Unconditional Self-Love we can't reach the goal of loving others unconditionally! You are truly amazing and have never given up the personal battle. I watched as you learned to forgive your own failings and value yourself, not material achievements which only measured your determination. Within, you journeyed into the darkest corners of yourself, which previously you never wanted to visit! And you triumphed, when you decided to face every frightening thought and feeling with compassion. You squared up, toe to toe with Anger, looked it in the eyes, studied it and then with loving intentions sent it away! You knew it was not for your highest good, and served no purpose, other than to make you feel like a bad person. But bad person you are not, good person you are! I notice Fear still bangs on your door occasionally, but when finding only love at home, it leaves as it's not the party it wanted to attend! Oh, and judging others! You sent judgements packing, like that imposter Fear telling you not to bother, it would be too hard and you'd never succeed, what a liar Fear is!!

Never belittle your tremendous efforts over the years, to do so would devalue yourself, and you'd fail to see true you. You are brave, Honest Sincere Wise and Courageous. How you ever got this far, through so many hurdles? shows you to be a tenacious force for good! You sought within and found what you were seeking, a place most fail to look!

When I look at you my friend, I see a light which gets brighter every day! A light that shines into the darkest corners of the World. In your presence a Soul feels drawn towards the light, like a Moth to a flame! Keep shining my good friend, never forgetting your quest for Love light and truth. I promise you, all will be well! Peace and Love will ever be at your side. Joy shall rise from within, Bright as the Stars and warmer than the Sun.

Namaste

From one who knows.

POETRY

PREFACE

Diamond in the Stone

"Diamond in the Stone" combines my first Book "A Life Worth Living" written in 2017 with my poetry, combined now entitled "Diamond in the Stone". My Biographical book is written as a consequence of my life experiences, which were sometimes difficult but inspirational to myself and others. My Poems outline how I awoke, and restored my connection with the natural and Human world via forgiveness, meditation, detachment, non-judgmental love for myself and others.

My intention is to inspire and encourage the reader to pursue the journey of seeking the inner *"Kingdom"* mentioned many times by the master. To a true seeker the promise "all things will be added unto thee" is real! And you will find this hidden jewel as I did!

Writing Poetry has been a *"revelation"* to me in every sense of that word! my pen appeared to write of its own volition! Each time I picked up my pen, I thought of the first word, the rest as they say is *"History"*! Words came flowing, not just any words, but the correct words summing up and rhyming, like water flowing from a tap! Straight from my heart. Wow! It was then I remembered the Biblical promise *"take no thought of the things which I should speak, but it would be given to me in that very hour, the words of which I should speak"* (King James Bible. Mathew 10:19) I was and still am truly amazed!

Like the reader, I have lived my life seeking to be happy and at peace, but found no lasting happiness or peace in things, places or

People. That's not to say things, people and places have not given me happiness and pleasure, but now my peace and happiness comes from within! My life before my awakened consciousness possessed no true meaning for me. It never made any sense to me, to be born then die!? But always the question of *why?* has directed me to work among the living and the dying as a registered Nurse. Prison Rehabilitation Counselor and Advisor. Homelessness Hostel worker and Police forensic Health Care Nurse. I had experienced life on the Streets from a young age (16 years old) allowing me to see into the lives circumstances, a nobody living in dark corners not usually seen by the general public.

I believe the joys and struggles of beings regardless of separation titles gave me the insight that we are all subject to difficulties, experience fleeting happy events, sadness and fears. The common denominator is "the human experience" which is pretty much the same for all of us. Whether in Prisons, Hospitals, Hostels, suffering homelessness death or hardships, we all feel fear sadness love or loss, when we are cut we bleed, we all respond to one extent or another in the same manner, therefor we are more one than separate!

My search for true and lasting peace has led me (unexpectedly) to look in a place I thought not to look inside of myself! I have heard it said *"if you want to hide something where no one will find it, hide it in plain sight"*! I had wandered what Jesus meant by the *"straight and narrow way"* and the *"kingdom within"* and *"seek ye first the kingdom"* but never realized he was pointing to the fact that all peace and every good thing lays within! *"to find yourself, you must first lose yourself"*! But as simple as it may sound, *"losing oneself"* or *letting go of me I and mine* or *"becoming as a child"* or *"becoming one"* and *"loving thy neighbor as thyself"* are contrary to everything we are educated / conditioned to believe from our parents, schooling, culture, and "the winner is best" mentality of our material competitive Societies norms!

Very few of us *"consider the Lilies of the field"* or the *"birds of the air"* Very few are *"one"* with the all! My biography and poetry is my journey to becoming *"one"* finding the way, the how of Love. There are many Gifts and wonderful blessings waiting for the honest seeker *"but few there be that find them"*

    I have found the way the truth and the life. I hope my journey and poetry may assist you in finding "the kingdom within" the path to that Diamond is the greatest adventure and treasure you will ever find..........

Diamond in The Stone

The Journey to Awakening
In the beginning
I heard an Angels voice
Seeking
Change going to come
Compulsive thinking
Billy and Barney two Zen cats
Creating my Reality
Acceptance
Identity
Time
The Power given to the Past
Wake up!
What is Now?
Detachment
Fear
Rising Sun
Comfort Zone
Snowfalls
Sleepless in the Night
Be Now!
Here Now and Now is Gone!
Become ye as a Little Child
Now in Silence
The Travelling Universe
Be The Watcher
Alchemy
Anger
Attachments

Mystery of Fear
What are Lies?
The World Within
The Human Body
The Effects of Unseen Energies
Energy of the Trees
The Mind- A Servant not the Master
Spark of Life
Human Mind Insanity
The Earth Trembles
The Journey
Let the Past Go!
Waiting
The Mind Trap
"Me" "I" and "Mine"
Only Now is Real!
I'm Late!
Captain Speaking
Arrival in Paradise
A New Day
Out of Body Journeys
The Higher Self
The Master "Consider the Lilies of the Field"
Magic
Prison Planet Earth
The Connection
Life surrounds All things
My Special Friend
When Death comes calling
Hidden Energies
A Body of Flesh
The Brain
Satori
The Secret

Prisoner of the Mind
Once upon a Stone
Impossible Life
Insanity of the Mind
Living Power
No Time!
Creating Gaps
Like Jesus and the Buddha
Awake
I awoke and Declared Freedom
Being Love
Unique R U
Say goodbye to you!
The imposter called "Ego"
"become ye as a Little Child"
Apple Tree
The young Prisoner
The Swamp
The Event
"He cried"
Don't strive after the Wind!
No Resistance!
Addictions
"Know ye not, that ye are Gods"
No more separation
"my Father, and your Father"
Windows
He healed me!
King Queen Villain Thief
Experiencing your Awakening signs!

The Journey to Awakening

Amazing views
Await you
Deep within the mind
In the Hidden place
Where only few can find!

"Is it worth the Journey"?
A friend once asked of me
In a quiet voice
I replied
"You will find your Destiny!"

He followed
searched within himself
Treasures Free from care
Astonished and Amazed
He found….
He was waiting there!

So if you begin this journey
The journey to your Soul
Be persistent
honest and true….
Awakened
You'll be Whole!

Ahead of you
Adventure
A journey

into Now
I Wish you "Namaste"
my Friend
Higher self will show you how!

Where
Awareness goes
Energy flows
Fears will subside.
Breath flows and Energy goes
Your Heart will open wide

In The Beginning

Beginning of our Journey
Cool on New Born Skin
From warmth and Comfort
Of the Womb
A New Life to Begin.

Exposed at once
To Cold Grey Life
Pure and full of Light
Colors not yet clear
to our Newborn sight

Life beginning
Awakened
by the chill on Soft Warm skin
Feeling the Warmth of Mothers Arms
We nestled safe within.

The Journey
had begun
Into the World of
Physical Life
Presented with
Illusion….
Of Fears
and the Strife!

I Awakened
At My Birth

again
at Future Time
First to Physicality
Then
to Life Divine!

I Heard an Angels Voice

One night
I heard an Angel
calling me by Name!
My Heart was filled with Love
I would Never to be the same.

I saw no Face
No shining Light
But I felt its presence sure
All Fears left my being
My Heart Alive once more!

Voice was quiet deep within
My name gently spoken
I'd longed to hear
that sweet small voice
Who knew
my Heart was broken!

And from that Night
My Life grew Bright
All Obstacles
came to view
But the memory of
that Sweet small voice
Again
My Strength did renew!

Several times
My Angel returned
calling me by name
When I was sad or lonely
When My Heart was
filled with Pain!

"Thank you my Angel"
You appear and you Know!
With Still Small Voice
You Call me
by my Name below

Seeking

I've looked in many places
For Answers to my Life
In Riches distractions
all I found was Strife

I began to look at others
In a World of Suffering
The Lost Dying and Lonely
But Peace
It did not bring

Remembering
The words of a Master
"Seek within and Find"
"the Kingdom"
you will discover
Peace and Love
beyond the Mind!

In order for us
"to enter in"
Stop
Minds constant Chatter!
"Be Still" and "Knock"
"Seek and find"
All that is
To matter!

What was the Gift
that I found?
That mattered
Most of all?
It was
the Gift
of Love
To share with one
and all!

"Change Going to Come"

Earth is Now Changing
Hidden to be Revealed!
The Awakening
is unfolding
to All
will then be Sealed!

Nothing will stop
The Change is Sure!
Heavens and Earth
Will Cry
"No more"!

Energy Flowing
From Heaven
to Earth
Revealing to all Hearts
Their Value
And their Worth!

"One Day"
we were told
"A New Heaven and new Earth"
So be ready
It is Here
About to give
New Birth!

With Birth comes the Pain
Of New Life
Just Begun
Be Ready
It is coming
with the Changing
of the Sun!

All Hearts
will be Changed
In the "Twinkle of an Eye"
none will be missed
Not you,
nor even I!

A Great Pulse of Light
Down from Heaven
From above
Will change every Heart
To Compassion
And to Love!

If the Lights Resisted
Great Pains will ensue!
Love will ensure
The Right Place
For me and You!

No Surprise
When that day Nears!
Signs above
Will tell us!
Fill your Hearts with Love
Let go all the Fears!

Compulsive Thinking

Gibbering Jabbering
Intellects
Endlessly
Darting here and there
Thoughts of Nothingness
Stop them if you Dare!

But "how" you ask?
"How do I stop"?
"I need my mind so badly"!
"Even when It drives you Mad"?
I ask
"Yes"!
You answer Sadly!

"Without my thoughts, who am I?
What would be left behind?
Alone! would I be worthless?
Without my Gibbering Jabbering Mind"?
Begin to Watch the thoughts
Look as they unwind
But pay them no Attention
No more Power they will find.

Don't let yourself be Prisoner
Captured by your Mind
Just begin to Watch your thoughts
Freedom you will Find!

No more Gibbering Jabbering Din
No more Dictator Mind Will Win
Serenity Peace Now Posses
You are the Power
The Mind is NOW
Much Less!

"Become ye as a Little Child"
No higher Mindedness
"Cease ye from all Judgement"
Giving Love
And true Kindness!

Billy and Barney

2 Cats
Sat side by side
Wise like two Zen Masters!
"Please, no Noise
Drama or Din
Can't you see we're Resting?
Peacefully within"

"Too much Noise
Too much Clatter
Don't Destroy our Peace!
Take a leaf from our Book
Let your Chatter Cease"!

"Now, away with you
And Please
Reduce the Noise!
Yes, we'd rather lay here
Than Play with all your Toys"

Within the Peace of Silence
Nothing does Perturb
The "Me, how" withdraws its Powers
Its Demands
Cannot Disturb!

In The Peace of Silence
No "could" nor "should"
or "wants"

They no Longer Scream
Like Spoiled
Brats and Debutants!

Occasionally
Two Cats Peek for food
From their hooded Eyes
For fresh treats to munch on
For such they'll Enterprise!

Creating my Reality

Creating my Reality
here in this Duality
Love or Judgements
Resistance Stances
I Create my Now's
No Coincidences?

By Act of Will
Setting an Intention
I Decide how I will Fare
My journey of Ascension

Not by Chance
Do I arrive
At my Destination
Predetermined Selflessness
Will Determine my Creation!

Rich or Poor
Old or Young
All a State of Mind!
We Choose
thoughts or Judgements
Of Love
or Words Unkind

Be not Deceived
Nor let Ego be your Master

Determine your Response
To Fortune or Disaster!

Have no Doubt
Naught by Chance
Outcomes
Rely on You!
Predetermine in Advance
What you'll think
And what you'll Do!

Acceptance

Fight the Now
if you will
Resist with all your Might
This Promise I will give you
You will Never Win the Fight!

The Harder That You Try
The more you're sure to Fail
Until you Stop Resisting
Allow Now to Prevail!

Go with the Peaceful Flow
Feel only Calm within
No Raging Battles anymore
Serenity you will Win

Resistance to the Present Now
Guarantees your Loss
Let it Go Let it be
It's time that Bridge to Cross!

The more that you Accept
And Let the Present Be
Welcome it
With Acceptance
Then you will be Free!

The Mind Habitually
Resists the Now

Finds The Now
A Threat!
But once Awareness
Sees It
Your Victory it is Set!

The Greater Part of all our Pain
So Unnecessary!
A Self-made Hell
By Insane Mind
Making Hearts
grow ever Weary.

Identity

More Identity with the Mind
More we are to Suffer
Let Minds Thoughts
Pass you By
The Now
You will Discover!

The Mind Resists
Living in The Now
But it is an Imposter!
Hear See and Feel this Now
All Beauty Heart Will Foster!

Minds Victory
It has Vowed!
Give Victory No More!
Taking Power Back
Live in The Now
Once More!

Mind Needs Time
Future Past!
Please Accept the Gift
By Awareness of This Present Now
Future Past
Will Drift!

No Past
No Future

Let it Cease!
"Live Your Life Right Now"
Let Time Awareness
Pass you By
Heart will show you How!

Time

I asked the Birds
"what Time is It"?
Trees and Plants
"What Day"?
All replied as One
"It's Now"
"Can't be no other way"!

Time Separates
Us from Now
Severed "Now's" Connection!
To get Now back
"Let Time Go"!
Then See the Now Perfection!

By giving
All Attention
To the One Cloud
In the Sky
Contour Shape and Breeze
Of that Cloud
Passing by!

Then you
Will Have Ears that Hear
Eyes that Really See!
A Heart that Truly Feels
Connected
You will Be!

The Power Given to the Past

Without
The Power of Living Now
The Past Remains in You!
Its Memories and its Pain
Still Occupies
You True!

The Child the Boy
the Man
All Hurts and Wrongs Attached!
With Chains Unbroken
Imprisoned Still
The Mind All Peace
Has Snatched!

Awake Allow your Now
See how Bright You Shine!
Peace will be
Your Precious Prize
If your Now
You don't Decline!

Suffering of the Child
Its Pain Screams Out Somehow!
Emotions of the Past
Don't Live
In our True Now!

Let all Go
Let it Pass
Forgive all Hurt and Pain
Start to Live in this "Your Now"
You will Never be the same!

Only Now, Holds the Key
To your Ball and Chain!
<u>Be in Now</u>
Don't Suffer
Daily Living all your Pain!

Wake up!

Wake up
Live in the Now
Now resolves the Pain!
Wake up and see the Now
Become "Whole" Again!

Bring your Burdens to the Light
Its Weight Will Rise Away!
From you with loving Gentleness
As in the Now You Stay!

Awake, no longer In the Dark
In the Now is Bright!
Here you Find the Darkness
Has transmuted
Into Light!

And in that Light Your Pain Expose
And Hide Away No more!
Truly you will have Found the Key
To Open your Now Door!

In Now
The Loves Bright Energy
Descends on all that's Dark
Brings Healing to your Heart and Mind
Leaving not a Mark!

What is Now?

What is in this Moment?
You can Watch It Curiously
Truly see it
Fully Accepting
It is What is will Be!

Life's Trapped and Lurking Energy
In the Darkness of your Deep
Will rise into the Light of Now
No longer will you Keep!

Bring all into the Light of Now
From Darkness
To Escape!
Watch it as its Reformed
The Now will it Reshape!

What is Now "Let it Be"!
From Minds War Refrain
Never! Let the Past and Future
Rise in You Again!

Then Marvel
How Life Will Change?
For Good and all The Betters
Living in the Now
Freed from all your Fetters!

Detachment

Disidentify
emotional Past and Pain
It Really Isn't You!...
Just Observe
its Friendship
Don't be tempted to Renew!

"The Watcher" Does not Say a Word!
In Silence It Retreats
No Argument, no Judgements
No Criticisms or Repeats!

Serenely the Observer
Its Weapon Strongest Love
Conquers all the hidden Hurts
Light Descends from up Above!

Yes, Dis Identify
All Judgement and Reproof
Just Watch without Opinion
Stay Peacefully Aloof!

Then, in Peace your War is Over
You are the Victor Sure
By and by
all Subsides
And "Now" will be your Cure!

Fear

Fear, where do you come from?
Silently you Creep
Through every crevice of the Mind
And Often Very Deep.

Nervousness
Un ease
And our Nightmare Dreads
Devoid of concrete Danger!
Beginning in our Heads.

Where does the Imposter Fear?
Gain its Mighty Strength?
Stopping us in our Tracks
Taking away
Our extra Length!

The Things that
Just May Happen!
While in the Here and Now
The Mind is creating
Fears
Stopping us Somehow.

Mind Projecting Foreword
To a Story yet Untold
Fear Writing Chapters
That Never Will Unfold!

Because we Feel
So Vulnerable
In our World of Scarce and Lack
Hunger Divisions Toil
And Greed
Keep us Looking Back.

In a World
Of Scarce and Lack
Divisions Wars and Greed
The Human Mind Manipulated
By Mainstream Medias Seed!
Seed is sown
By Planters Dark
Fears Grow
Much Louder
Feeding off that Fear
The Planter Grows Much Prouder!

Can the Planters
Be Defeated?
All Fears to Erase!
"Yes they can"
If we as One together
Our Power
Will Amaze!

Make it
Our Life's Mission
To rid our World of Fear
Take our Power Back
Corruptions End is Near!

We Wrestle not
Flesh and Blood
But Powers Principalities
The Rulers of the Dark
In their Created Realities.

Rising Sun

Early Morning Rising
To the Sea and Sand below
I watched transfixed and Captured
By the Magical Yellow!

Higher and Higher
Bright and Clear
The Sun rose in the Sky
Sounds of Sea and Barking Strays
Each Peacefully Passing by.

Mind merged with Now
Absorbed transfixed as One
No Longer was I separate
From the Yellow Golden Sun!

I was the Wind
The Sea was Me
Crashing Splashing Ebbing and Flow
I Now knew there was much more
To my Life Below!

Gentle Cooling Wind
Soothed the Burning Sun
As I became at one with All
My awakening had Begun!

Seeing Within
The Hidden World
Truth Buried by the Mind
I began my Journey
What Else I would Find?

Comfort Zone

Moving out of Comfort Zone
Seeing through Veils Thin
I found Adventure Treasures Hid
My Child I found Within.

Seeking out the Wonder
Hidden by Daily Grind
Inner Eyes revealed to Me
The Magic of Mankind

Infinite Possibilities
All Futures came to Mind
My Heart grew ever Fonder
More Gentle and more Kind!

Pulling back the Curtain
I saw what was behind
Our Gifts had all been Hidden
By that Imposter
We call Mind!

Thrill of New Beginnings
In this present Now
Your Gift not yet Received
But Offered Anyhow!

Directions have been Given
From Masters New and Old
Where to Find your Connection
"Be Still"
Let all Unfold!

Snowfalls

White Geometry Falling
Stroking Earth so Lightly
Softly Caressing Leaves and Boughs
Breaks when it grows Mighty!

Each Bough
Clothed like a King
War cloak of brilliant White
Lays over the Child
Who Sang and Played
and in this World had Sight!

Birds call Sweetly
Life buried deeply
Beneath the falling Snow
Calling to all who may Listen
Non heard and never will Know!

Like calls heard Far in the Distance
Snow Flakes fall and they Fade
A Child Forlorn hungry
Dying
A Footprint in Snow
never made!

Snowfalls
and White together we see

Bullets are Fired
But Separation Says
"oh it's another
Not Me"!

Sleepless in the Night

Awoken by a Mystery Sound
Eyes searching in the Dark
Laying wide Awake
Ego begins to Bark!

Morning seems so Far away
Thoughts begin to Surface
Mind begins its Merry Dance
Ego builds its Case.

All Alone
With one's own Self
The Party can begin!
you wish it was the morning
You know you'll never Win!

The Mind
has you to its self
Identity You Can't Escape!
You have to lay and listen
No use
Gaffer Tape!

Are there Two
Laying in the Dark
The Speaker and the Hearer??
Am I the Mind?
And if so
Mind Hear my Orders Clearer!

If Commanded
"Mind be Still"
"Go to whence you came"
You'd still be laying
Wide Awake
All would be the same!

When morning
Then to you arrives
Blurry eyed and Tired
You scream from weary Heart
"Mind, how to Control?"
"Live Now, Then Mind Retired!

Be "Now"

Going on inside of You?
Do not analyze
Only Watch and See!
Thoughts and all Emotions
And the moving Energy.

With Urgency
We must declare
Our Sovereignty from the Mind
or Mind grows into Monster
That can Destroy Mankind

If Earths Home
We Destroy
Pursuing Wealth and Gain
How will Evolution
Return to Love
Insanity to Sane!

To Evolve from dense hard matter
Searching for the Light
One day it will happen
We will regain
Loves Sight

Here Now and Now is Gone

How can we ever Know?
When our Last Chance
has come?
To Know
How Precious
Our Now is
Before our Lives Are Done!

To Show
The Ones We Care for
How true is our Love?
Before we say
Our Last Goodbye
And return to
All above!

See the Now
With Heart and Eyes
The Smiles the Laughs
And Tears
Before your Now
It Passes
Gone like All the Years!

Will you
And I
Ever Know

Our Race it has been Run
When all our Now is Gone
Our Time on Earth
Is Done!

Become ye as a Little Child

"Become ye as a Little Child
Of Such is the Kingdoms Heaven"
Lay down
Your Lofty Mindedness
Each Day
From One to Seven

Put to Rest
Your Judgement
Away all Vengeful Thought
Learn to
Be at One with Now
Or Now
Will come to Naught!

The Now
Flies by each Moment
Never to Return
So get your Act Together
It is Now
You have to Learn!

See the Now
with Awe and Wonder
Hear the Birds in the Spring
If we become as a Child
Our Hearts like Thiers
Will Sing

A Child
Become
Then Now Will See
Every little thing!
Hearts will fill with Love
And Life to You
Will Bring!

Now in Silence

Within
The Now in Silence
Nothing does Perturb
The "I"
Withdraws its Power
The Mind Cannot Disturb!

In
The Peace of Silence
No Could
No Should
No Wants
Sneak around
Or Shout Aloud
Like Spoilt Brat Debutants

In
The Peace of Silence
No Ego
to be Heard
No Hurts
No Fears
No Vengeance!
Free
Just Like the Bird!

No
Me
No

I
No
This is Mine
Now only
Is Your Time!

Give your "I" Away
Let your "Me" no longer stay
Only Now Will Leave with you
On The Appointed Day

Now is the only Time
Truly Live Exist
"Seek and you will Find"
behind Illusions Mist!!

The Travelling Universe

Planets Stars Comets and Suns
All Travelling Constantly
Bringing Changes
Dark and Light
Through all Eternity

Unseen Forces
have their way
Venus Mars and Milky way
Gravity and the Gamma Ray
Magnetic Forces
On us Play.

Galaxies
Moving Endlessly
On Pre-Determined Course
Bringing to us all
Consciousness Awakening
From a Loving Endless
Source!

Repeated
Through Millennia
Each Change is Sure and True
The Arrival of Awakening
For the Writer and for You!

The Journey
Of our Universe

Nothing can Deter
The Fate of all Mankind
These Movements
Will Declare!

Lion
Will Lay down
With the Gentle Lamb
Swords turned into Plowshares
Stop it? No One Can!

Two may
Stand together
Only one will go!
When that Day Arrives
Only then we All Will Know!
Prepare All Hearts
Nothing will Stop
The Changes yet to Come.
When Peace on Earth Begins
from the Power
Of the Sun!

For our Natural State
Of Oneness
Taken from us at our Birth
Be Returned to all
That walk upon the Earth.

Our Being
Beyond our Name and Form
Is waiting to be Found
The Light of our True Self

The Knowledge that will
Astound!

Then we will Discontinue
from all our Mental Stream
Living in the Now
Awoken
as from a Dream

Every movement
Every Step
Breath of Life within
Conscious of The Now
The Now that
You are in!

Fully Present
In the Gift
This Gift
you might not Find!
Unless you Look within the Now
And the Silence of the Mind.

Be the Watcher

For when Watcher
Disappears Absent from its Care
Your Now it fades from view
To Find
Ego Waiting there!

When Master said
"Watch and Pray"
Heed all Wisdoms Words
"Why"? you ask, he replies
"Consider ye the Birds"

When Fears Cares Thoughts and Plans
Chase away the Watcher
Peace and Love
Takes their Leave
Signaling
Watchers True Departure!

Alchemy

"Magic"
Some they called it
Turning Metal into Gold
But Look Within
See the New
Changed from you of Old!

Taking Metal
Of Dark Emotions
"Now" transmutes the Poison Vial
Gold is "Now" Made
From the Festering
Decaying Pile!

"Esoteric"
You may say
"How do I Heed this Promise"?
By Kindness
Love towards Yourself
Don't be a "Doubting Thomas"!

As once your Freed
From all your Care
Life is Lived with Ease

"Sorry"
*if you misheard
I Did not say
"It would be a Breeze"!*

Anger

Anger
Ego's Weapon
Your Peace it will Destroy!
As hurtful words
And Vengeful thoughts
The Ego Will Deploy!

Beneath Your Anger
Born of Pain
Screams a Child whose Lost!
Allow this suffering to pass by
Consider What the Cost!

As
The Watcher
Observe and Learn
Anger is a Fraud!
When the Past
By Now Dissolved
You'll no Longer need a Sword!
So Battle
Not with Anger
Or take up Ego's Harm
Just Observe its Rise
"Now"
Rage begins to Calm!

Aware of Now
Dissolves

Past Pain
As Ego Loses Grip!
Letting go Resistance
From Loves Cup
You will Sip!
Become
You as that Little Child
Amazed and full of Wonder
All your Anger will abate
loses all its Thunder!

Attachments

Detach!
Expectations
Will No Longer
Rule your Life
Being Aware of Now
Let's Go
Minds Ego Strife

Clinging
On Dependently
To People and to Things
Doesn't add to Peacefulness
But only Drama brings!

Afraid
In Fear of our Loss
Feeds Attachment still!
But if we Learn
To Live in Now
Our Love of Life
Will Fill!
Desires
Needs and Grasping
Complicates our Lives!
Why not Free them
from their Bonds?
And watch as Peace Arrives

Relationships
Are Sweeter
Let those you Love
Be Free!
To Pursue their Peace
Their Happiness
Supporting them
To Be!

Trying
To Complete Ourselves
While Feeling Incomplete
Letting Now Releases You
From having to Compete!

Mystery of Fear

Fear
Where do you come from?
Silently you Creep!
Through every crevice
of the Mind
Often very Deep!

Nervousness
Tensions
And the Nightmare Dread!
Devoid of Concrete Danger
Beginning in our Head!

Where
Does this Imposter
Gain its Mighty Strength?
Stopping us in our Tracks
From going Extra Length!

Imagining
What Might Happen
While in the Here and Now
The Mind is in the Future
Creating Fears
In us Somehow?

The Mind
Projecting Foreword
To a Story not yet Untold

Fear Writing Chapters
That Never
Will Unfold!

Feeling Vulnerable
In a World
of Scarce and Lack
Hunger
Divisions
Greed And Toil
Keeps the Masses
Looking Back!
In our World
Of Scarce and Lack
Divisions Wars and Geed
Easily Manipulated
Planted by a Seed!

Seeds
Are Sown
By Planters Dark
Fears Grow Ever Louder
And Feeding off That Fear
The Planters
They Grow Prouder!

Can
These Planters Be Defeated?
Their Fears to Erase!
Yes! They Can
If We Together
The Banner of Love
We Raise!

Make it
Our Life's Mission
To Rid the World of Fear
Take our Power Back
The Planters time is
Near!

We Wrestle
Not with Flesh and Blood
But with Principalities
Against the Rulers of the Dark
In Created Realities!

What are Lies

What are Lies
But things with Wings
Cause Misery and Destroy
Lies
Must Stop
When realized
Lies
Can Steal Another's Joy

What
Are Lies
Those Vicious Words
Hunting to Deceive
Changing Time Lines
Of others
By those
Willing to Believe

The World Within

The World Within
Down to
Our smallest Atom
A Reflection
Of the Universe
Can we See?
Can we Fathom?

We can
When we Seek
The Higher Self within!
Only Seekers
Of the Truth
Can make this
Change Begin!

The Truth
Is Found
Within
"the Straight
And Narrow Way"
A Path
That Leads
You to
A Loving Bright
New Day!

The Master
Declared

"The Kingdom"
Only Found Within!
"Few there be"
Who Find It!

Then
Heart Mind
And Body
Will Hear See and Feel!
The Hidden Kingdom
Deep Within
Exposing
All
that's Real!

Radiating
From All Living!
Is a Light
Energy Aglow!
Go Within Look Without
See and Feel It!
Then You'll Know!

Connecting
With that Living Light
Fills your Being True!
Stronger Calmer
You'll Become
In Everything
You Do!

Relight
Your True Vision
See from Mind's

Forgotten Eye!
Bring to Life
Once Again
All Wonders
That Pass by!

And when
That Flame Within You
Ignites Your Inner Light
Connecting to All That Lives
You'll
See with Inner Sight!

Then with Clear Vision
Consider Birds and Trees
That "Nothing is Arrayed"
As Beautiful
As These!

Time
And Time
And Time Again!
It's been spoken
very True!
"Consider Lilies of the Field"
Let "Birds" come into View
The Promise of the Master
Will be
Revealed to You!

Home
We Have Longed for
Deep within our Heart
Is not this Time or Place!

But Where we
the "Angels Sang
For Joy"
Then from Home
Chose to part

When Change to Earth
And Human Kind
Rolls upon our Sphere
Our True Home
Will be Revealed
No longer
Will we Fear!

The Veils will part
And Sight Reveal
A dawning of New Day!
And each and All
In their New Home
Will make the Choice to Stay!

So "be still"
All fearful
beating Hearts
That Day will surely come!
All Fears
Doubts and Lack
Be melted by the Sun

The Human Body

Humans!
All our Wants
Causing Earths
Destruction!
Earth she Struggles
to Sustain
Grasping greed of Man
Our Dysfunction
of Consumption!

This Body!
Needs to Modify
Alter DNA
Human Form
Then Welcome
The New Evolving Day!

All Energy All Creation
Of Atom they are Formed
All the Light That enters in
All will be Reformed!
Light begin
To Change
"As above below"!
Allow the Light
by us to Shine
Begin to Grow and Glow!

Light will change the Needs
Of all Living Kind
Tomorrow
Will come
change
The Bodies
Of Mankind!

No more
Earths Destruction!
All creatures
will be Free!
Watch and Hope
And Prayer in Faith
That Day we all will See!

Many Lives have we Lived

Many Lives
we all have lived
Some more
than of Others
Kings and Queens
Warriors and Rogues
Fathers and Loving Mothers

The Soul
It enters our New Life
When Birth to us it gives
For an Instant
Knowledge Flows of a Soul
And Lives relived!

The Memory
starts to Fade Away
Of where we have come from!
But the Pain and Karma
of those Lives
Continues to Live on!
Each New Birth
began anew
To Try till soul Succeed
To reach that purpose long ago
In Dimensions We Decreed!
That we would find our way
to Love
The Deep and Endless Need!

First
To Learn to Love
Ourselves!
Then Cherish every Soul
Reaching purpose of our Lives
Become
Unified and Whole!

Rebirth and Death
Will Follow
Until the Lesson Learned!
When we arrive at Love
Our Kingdom
We'll have Earned!
Pearl of Great Price

Search for your Kingdom
But not outside!

Be ready to give up all
Cast your Net deep within
You will hear the Call!

A Treasure
Deep inside you
Which is truly Wealth!
To find it
You must seek the NOW!
Abandon all your stealth!

Hearts
that do not Feel
Ears that do not Hear
Will never find that Pearl
So Deep
Heavens Kingdom there!

Rich men
cannot Enter
Nor Thieves its Treasure Steal
Only as Little Children
Will Heavens Gifts reveal!

Imagination
Once revealed
Connects all Living Spheres
The Gate is Widely Opened
The Kingdom
Then Appears!

Seek the Kingdom
And its Treasure

See as it reveals
Hidden Secrets to the Few
By seeking
break the Seal!

The Effects of Unseen Energies

The Moon it shines on all the World
Calming Raging Seas
Sun Bursts out its Radiance
Can Burn or Warm with Ease!

Unseen by all the World
The Universe Sheds its Light
Bringing Change to People
To the Day
And to the Night

The substance of our Bodies
Affected by the Light
Decay or Growth
Brings Changes
To our Human Sight

The Water
And our Cellular World
All Substance due for Change
Hidden Energies from the Stars
Begins to Re arrange!

What will Change?
The question may be asked!
What will come to View?
No more Hidden Secrets
The Time is Now
And Due!

Energy of the Trees

Meditating near a Tree
Blissful Peace absorbed
Strength and Noble Frequency
My Body
Feels Restored!

A lasting
Exchange Taking Place
Between Elements of Existence
A Gift is given
A Gift Received
By Peaceful un resistance

The Mind
A Servant not a Master

Who is it
That Listens to the Mind?
When Mind is Silent
What is Heard?
What do we See?
We are Master
Of the Mind
When we
Silence all its Chatter!
Mind cannot Create
In Silence!
Listen to the Mind
Pay it no Attention!
Mind will Cease
And You will
Be the Master!

Spark of Life

The Spark of Life Resides
in all that we can See
Still your Mind
Connect your Heart
And at one you'll
Always Be!

A Plant
A Tree
A Pet
A Bird
Each contains our Being!
Look Truly Deeply
From your Heart
And Life
You'll Always See!

Human Mind Insanity

One Hundred and Twenty-Three Million
In Twentieth Century alone
Killed by Bombs
and Bullets
Now Names Carved into Stone!

Madness? Badness? Insanity? All of Human Mind!
Will the Killing Stop?
The Destruction Of Mankind!?

By Silence We give our Consent
For Leaders to Attack!
To take the Life of Millions Who Are Never coming back

False News from Main Stream Media
Calls to us Each Day Dividing Human Consciousness
"The others have to Pay"
We can End It Here and Now!
By taking back our Powers
Becoming One with All
The Birds the Trees and Flowers!

Ideas in The Mind

Our Mind Speaks to us
"Everything's OK"
But somewhere deep inside of us
We don't Believe It!

Dis Ease
Is here to Stay!

But that Resistance
To the Truth
That Truly We Are Free!
Freedoms just a Thought away
"Let the Now just be"

The Past is Gone
Future yet untold!
Why fill each Now
With Dis Ease
Let your Peace
In Now Unfold!

The Earth Trembles

Shaking off the Pains of Wars, Hurt and Greed of Man
Let's bring Peace to Mother Earth
Let's do it While we can!

Earths Healing Held within our Hands
Will bring about Release! No more Hunger Wars or Fears
Nurture Love and Peace!

Anxiety Stress and Fear Just let them all Go!
I promise "you won't miss them"
And Peace to you will Flow!

When that Peace to all Mankind Delivers our Salvation
Earth will Sing the Song of Love
To All and Every Nation.

Caressed and Soothed by Human Hearts
Earth Grows Still and Calm
Nature Blooms More Radiantly, Fed by Psychic Balm!

The Journey

We Often Hear "The Journey not the Destination"
But "The First Step is the Hardest"
And requires Determination!

"Don't you bother" Ego says "It's really not worth the Effort"
But doing Something, Anything!
Demands that we Exert!

But you say "Life has given me nothing,
only Heartache and Regret"
"And if I try but don't succeed, why should I bother yet"!

Because my Fellow Traveler
To you I say and Sure "Enjoy each Arduous Step"
You will find that Open Door!

That Door Will Open Widely
And Beckon Loud to You
And Every Desired Goal
Your Heart will see you Through!

Let the Past Go

Sadness Reactions and Anger
The Energies of the Past!
Become a Bottomless Pit
Holding You in Steel Grasp!

The more you Dwell in the Past
More will come to View!
So Why Not Stop your Thinking
Then Now will come to You!

When No more Future Past Survive
To Now You Arrive
You find True Self
And Enjoy
The Thrill of Being Alive!

Alive your Consciousness
Liberated you will be!
Let Go the Past and Future
The Now You'll Learn to See!

Waiting

Living in the Now, not looking back or forth
Requires Total Awareness
The Now All Effort Worth
If something happened in your Now
And you are not Awake
You will miss "The Event"
Of this Make no Mistake!

The Arrival of the Change
We then can see it all
And Welcome the Event
When it comes to call!

All Light and Frequency
Will greet who in present are
The Body Will Transfigure
Like A Distant Nova Star!

Be Alert Still and calm, Awaiting the Arrival
When all will Know that being present
Will Determine our Survival

The Mind Trap

In Pursuit of Physical pleasures
To help Free from Fear and Dread
To Feed a Mind Ever Grasping
To fill an empty Bed!

When I get the things I want, Then Happy I will Be
But do not be Deceived my Friend
No Happiness will you see!
For in Illusions Trickery
And Attachments of all Kind
You will only find momentary Pleasure
And Grasping of the Mind!

Needing Wanting Seeking
Your Mind your Master Be! Don't look outside, search within
And always you'll be Free!

If Peace beyond Understanding
You wish with all your Heart
Feel this Now, Invite it in
This now's the Place to Start!

"Me" "I" and "Mine"

If Heavens True Dimensions you wish to Enter In
Drop "me" and "I" and this is "Mine"
Then Heaven you will Win!

Imagine Life without these Chains of "Me" and "I" and "Mine"
"Let them go, set them Free"
Stop wasting precious Time!

And as the Veils across your Eyes, to Free you from them All
Your Vision starts to Clear
Freedom from the Fall!

Starting from that Moment, See Feel and Hear!
The Natural Music all around
You will stop and Stare!

A Magic spell on you is cast, Revealing Hidden Sight
In Awe and Wonder you will walk
Now your Moments Bright!

Only Now is Real

Obsessing Past and Future, reliving Ghostly tread
Wishing Desiring Wanting
Thoughts inside your Head!

But only Now is truly Real, all we ever Live!
Why not make the most of it? to Now
Attention give!

Past or Future don't be concerned, they have no place in Now!
The Present surely is a Gift
You'll be Amazed
Somehow!
When your Now it comes to stay, forever to Abide
Caressing you with Love
Constant by your side!

So Seek and Search, don't give in!
One Day an outstretched Hand
Will draw you in, and Show you
Earth is the Promised Land!

I'm Late!

Several lay Dead at the scene
"Late late late we'll be"
No time to Care or Feel!
Only Time do we Care about
Nothing else is Real!

Souls are gone, but we are here!
Looking at our Watch
They are Free, we remain
Time continues on its March!

Like the March Hare Screaming long
"I'm late for an important date"
The Dead no longer tell the Time
"It could have been our Fate"!

Captain Speaking

Captain on the Speaker
"we're cruising at 34,000 feet!
We're flying into Turbulence
Please remain in your seat"

Captain on the Speaker
"Please heed no Smoking Rule
I know some may be Nervous
I don't mean to be Cruel"

Captain on the Speaker
"Sorry about my tone
Please ensure your Phones on Flight mode
No, you can't call Home"

"Captain on the Speaker
Please sit down, relax
Feel Free to walk the Narrow Isle
Stretch your Aching Backs"

Captain on the Speaker
"We've just had a Complaint
Telling us your Angry
At our Passenger" Restraint

Captain on the Speaker
"a Man was trust up tight
Beaten up by Cabin Staff
he attacked them in Mid-flight"

Captain on the Speaker
"Get back in your seat
Or I'll come out there
With Pepper Spray
Then you'll feel the Heat"

Passengers to the Captain
"Please stop we're getting out
We've had enough of sitting still
What's this all about"

Passengers to the Captain
"We hear Customer is King
We've been up several Hours
And you've called us everything"

"So Stop the Plane
And set us Down
And don't forget our bags
No more of our rudeness
Sorry we're all such Nags"

Passengers to the Cabin Crew
"Remember it's our Cash
That keeps you in your Holidays
So do not be so brash!

"So remember Airliners
With all your fancy bling
Its Passengers that Pay your Rent
We truly are your King"

Arrival in Paradise

The Sun was hot and baking
The Natives stopped to Stare
"Hello Mr. and Mrs. Tourist
A Dollar can you spare"?
Smiling back Politely
Pretend we didn't see
The rows of Pearly Whites
Saying "Money give to me"

At last arriving at our stay
And shown to our Big Room
No Water! No Electric!
But told
"would be here soon"!

The Natives
they were Friendly
Invited us for Tea
We asked where was the Toilet?
"Round the back if we had to Pee"!

A Smiling Native calls to me
"Come see Wares for Free"
I will Polish Nails
And Massage you
"Come Missy
For a Dollar
Your Friend I will be"!

Missy, my man is a Bad Man
He beat me and take Drug!
come with me to Market
We Play Music
Then drink Jug!

Replying "no my Sister"
We think the Truth is Hid!
This Now is so amazing
But here
have a Quid!

A New Day

Birds are sweetly Singing
Sky is Azure Blue
No Mind
Is so Beautiful
Only Now comes to my View!

Peaceful watching Clouds unfold
Life feels like a Feast
Pen Hovers over page
Moving West to East!

Words Flow
With so much Ease
Gliding like a Bird
Flowing
From my Heart
Where Each and all
are spurred!

Out of Body Journeys

From top of Head
To tip of Toes
Where Intention is
Energy Flows
From Crown
To Mother Ghia
I Radiate my Love
Sending and Receiving
Light from up Above
Third Eye
Now is open
Visions Now They Show
Sacred Geometry
From where
I do not Know?
Faces so Familiar
Passing by so Slow
From where
I don't Remember
But I know
I do so know!
Where are the Energies
Of Lives gone by?
Memories of Pasts
and Futures
Drift in and out of Mind
Of Green Pleasant Pastures
Floating above
Seas and Hills

Gliding so much Fun
Once again Returning
to my Mind
when Spirits Journey Done!
Never wanting
to return
But Mind
Again Aware!
In Meditation
I will Fly
Soar without a Care

The Higher Self

It is True
That Deep within
We have a Higher Self!
Who awaits our Soul connection
Here lies the Promised wealth

When once
We gain the entrance to the Door
Not yet opened wide
Our entrance to the Hidden World
On the other side!

On entering in
Our Eyes renew
Then We see the hidden view
What lays there? I hear you ask!
What is hidden from my Gaze?
The Masters Promised Blessings
Sights that will Amaze!

So Continue on your Journey
Until you reach the shore
Where Visions of your Now
Reveal Angels
And much more!

In the Silence Calm and Tender
The Hidden Truths Revealed

There a World Awaits
Where Promises Are Sealed!

Deep in Heavens Halls
Awaiting Seekers of the Truth!
Enter in and Pass by
You who have sought in Silence
Some from young
And Tender Youth!

"Choose you this Day"
Be Here, or be There!
You who have arrived
Will climb
that Golden Stair!

Now you See
As you are Seen!
"As above so below"
Your Journey to the Promised Joys
All Blessings you will Know!

No more
Physical Barriers!
Your Wings have Spread
Now Fly!
Into the New Dimensions
Above Beyond
The Sky!

The Master
("Consider the Lilies")

Master Jesus taught us well
how to seek the Kingdom?
"Be still and Love"
Letting go
To you be given
Wisdom

Some asked the Master
"How do we enter in"?
Letting go of all Attachments
The only way to Win!

No "Rich man"
Worldly
Striving to be Great!
Can enter in to the Kingdom
Only by Love
And the "narrow Gate"!

"Come follow me"
And "seek"
The "Living Flame"!
The Holy of Holy's awaits you
You will Never be the same"

"Whether in or out the Body!
You will see
Why the Master came?

You will see Truths Reality
You will never be the same!

The Master instructed "the Kingdom"
Hidden deep within our Hearts
Can be found by
"Seeking" "Knocking" "Asking"
Then Heaven to us
imparts!

And once we see that "Precious Gift"
No force of Will can hold!
A "Gift" Indeed
Can't be Bought or Sold!

So, is it worth the Journey?
The Long and Narrow Way!
"Oh, yes my Friend
Reach out
You are so much more
Than Clay"!

Magic

Astrology Numerology
Sacred Geometry
Each reveal their Truths
Around you are many Proofs!

All of Life Is Governed
By the Heavens up above
The Geometry of all Life Revealed
When your Heart is Filled with Love

The Frequency of Heaven
The Shuman Resonance!
Determines Evolutions Time
Nothing is by Chance!

One Day when
Frequency is Changed
The Awakening will begin
Animals Plants and All Mankind
In Light all bathed within!

The Frequency
Of all Atoms
Will change and resonate
A New Beginning
Yet imagined
All Truth Emanate!

Our Higher being
Awaits to hear our call
by your side
Abide with you
And show the Hidden All!

Released
Unfettered by our Chains
Each will dwell in Peace
Freed from Hunger Wars and Greed
All Hidden Secrets Cease!

Prison Planet Earth

Some have said
"Earths is a Prison Planet"
Divided from all others!
we Learn
"the Golden Rule"
How to Love
All others

When at Last
We have Learned
that simple perfect Rule
Galactic Travelers we will meet
From the Universal Pool!

Awaiting there
Among the Stars
They see us from afar
They dare not come any Closer
I know it sounds
Bizarre!

But would you come
Within a Mile
Of a Planet
Drenched in Blood?
Facing a Deadly Weapon
Pointing where you stood!

So they
Stop and wait awhile
Watching our kind Kill!
Each other
and their Children
Until we've had our Fill!

The rule of all Galactic Folk
Cease from useless Strife
"Do no Harm" to Planet
Do no harm to Life!

Will they wait forever
Or will it come to Pass?
laying all our weapons Down
The Golden Rule alas!
The Reality
of ET's presence
The Evidence
Does Convey!
Statesmen
Declare
the Truth
In denial
Will we
stay?

Slowly
ET's Technology
Will surface
To our view
But Oil
Controls
Our Planet

To the
Benefit
Of
the Few!

Sickness
Disease
Wealth and
Power
Of
Elites
One Day will End!
As Truth
Will take
From Them
Their Thrones
No more
Defend!
So
While
We Wait
And watch
Tears from
Children Flow
ET Bides
Their time
One Day we all will Know!

The Connection

Staring out into the Crowd
At People Passing by
Each turning back to look
Do you ever wonder Why!

What is this Connection
That makes them turn about?
What is it they are sensing?
That impels them to
Find out!

Some say we have sixth Sense
Hidden from our View!
Letting us Know Instinctively
What Another's going to do!

A sudden Fear of Danger
Warns our Dormant Mind
Of things our Eyes can't see
A Mystery of our kind!

So might it be
We all can't see
That each possess the Gift?
A long forgotten Secret
Of a Soul who's set Adrift

Can this Secret Gift Be Found?
Our Ability Renewed!

Yes, it can if Mind is Tamed
To This Jesus did Allude!

When our Minds they are Free
From the Collective Insanity!
Hidden Gifts then be seen
Freed from Mankind's Vanity!

All around will feel your Heart
All around your Stare!
Deepest Hidden Secrets
Your Burdens and your Care!

When your Gifts to you
Who have sought the Masters ways
To you who's Hearts have Opened
Who Follow Loves Lights Rays!

You who walk in Light
Remembering Masters Words
"Greater things shall you do"
Gifts all to you Transferred!

Never Doubt
Never Fear
Once you Know the Truth!
Each Cell of your Body
Becomes Fountains of Youth!

When Master said "Come Follow Me"
It was a call to All!
So be the Love, be the Light
Never will you Fall!

Life Surrounds all Things!

Sparkling Lights
A Crown surrounds the Tree
Shimmering points of Energy
When we Learn to See!

Each Plants Surrounding Aura
Will come into your View
When you connect your Essence
The Elementals speak to you!

Only by Loves Energy
Can you see the Light!
Surrounding all Living things
By Day and Darkest Night!

If Magic, you really wish to see
Then don't delay no more!
Enter in the Narrow Gate
Through the Open Door!

How Sad and Tragic it would be
When at the End of Life
You had missed the Magic
only Toil and Strife!

"Come follow me" the Master called
Loud for all to Hear!
But Few there be who choose to find
The Hidden Magic There!

"The Kingdom" Jesus said
Lays Deep within your Hearts
"Seek and ye shall find"
The Light Universe Imparts!

If at Special moments
You see and catch a glance!
The Loving Energies surrounding Things
Know, this not by Chance!

When your Sight you have Regained
You might ask
"How did I become so Blind"?
You chose to Forget!
But said "you would Seek and
you would Find"!

You knew that when you awoke
You would be whole once more!
the journey would be Hard
But would find that open Door!

You knew, New Earth New Heaven
Would be returned once more
All the Wondrous Gifts Restored
Hidden Never more!

What is the Path?
What is the Way?
Where is the Open Door?
Where do you Seek?
Where do you Find?
So Heaven Can Restore!
"I am the Way

I am the Light
I am the Truth Divine
Drink my Living Waters
Your change will be my Sign"!

My Special Friend

My Special Friend remained with me
When I was young and Pure!
But when my Mind was Darkened
They dwelt with me no more!

Becoming like a Child
Is Easier said Than Done!
Requires strength of Will
Releasing
What was Fun!

By Ego and Divided Mind
We Lose the Child within
Yet it waits to be Restored
But we must let it in!

Seek you to become that Child
Find the Joy in All!
When Life feels Like a Burden
At such times you must Call!

When Death comes Calling

When Death it comes Calling
When it's my time to Soar
No Fear of its Presence
It's just an Open Door!

With Open Arms and Gladness
A little Sadness too!
I will walk through that Open Doorway
Into a world I knew!

How can I know what lays beyond?
This I know is True!
I've been through that door before
And No Fear is Death Due!

Death where is thy Sting?
Grave where is they Care?
For in that moment my Body Passes
A New gown I will wear!

This corruptible fleshy sack
In Twinkle of an Eye
Shall put on immortality
And yes, again I will Fly!

Locked in Time

Locked in Time
But all it ever is
Is Now!
Capture it and Enjoy
Immerse yourself and Wow!

Take no thought of Tomorrow
Or that which passed you by
The Moment Now
That you're in
To "It" bid your biggest "Hi"!

And Now will greet you in return
Bid you fond Welcome
No second moment will arrive
The Now is never done!
Give Now full attention
Feel and Hear and See
Now is gone by the time you think of it
So in the moment be!

Hidden Energies

Hidden Energies
all around
Moon pulls in the Sea
Atoms Frequencies
In everything are near

Surrounded by such Energy
Why are non for Free?
To power our Homes
Link our Minds
get each
From A to B

Surrounded
in
As without
Something does
not sit right with me
Where has all the Power gone
Why is it not for Free?

A Body of Flesh

Looking in my Mirror
What is it I see?
A Body of Flesh
Staring
Curiously
Looking back
At me!

Is the "I"
That's Looking
The same
As "I am"
Or
Is the "I"
That is seeing
Like a Snail or Clam?

When "I" Hear My Mind
Thinking Thoughts Not Chosen by "I am"
Who is doing the Talking if "I am" is Listening
Who is Talking to Who
If the Body I wear
is not my true being?
Like a Snail with its home in a Shell
Then who is powering my Vehicle
It's all Crazy as Hell!

When Mind
Silenced by Silence

I look at this Body and Ask
Do I need you
To carry on Living?
Or Beyond my Form
Is there another Task?

For a very Short Period
"I am"
Lives within
This Body
With the Clatter of the mind
Its unceasing Din!

The Brain

The Brain
Constantly chatting
Thinking it is Boss!
Until the
"I am"
Notes the Noise
Then thoughts Power
They are Lost!

When you tell
Your thoughts your Servants
immediately be Quiet
Brain Fights back
refuses
Causes such a Riot!

In Charge of this Body
Is your "I am" Commander!
Choose "I am" to steer your Ship
Bid Mind "be Still" quit all its chatter
then True Destiny you will Fulfill!
"I am"
Is listening Observing
To all as it passes by
All that to you is Now Happening
By Body by Mind and Eye!

Let the Observer
Without Judgement or Care

Watch as all Passes by
Do not analyze or Critique
Outcomes
arrive by and by!

Soon you will be
a Person of Light
Walking by Heart
Not by Sight!

"It will pass" A Sage once said to me
Head bowed on my Bended Knee
He Taught me to be Now
be still detach then I will be Free!

Satori

"Satori"
Flash of Insight
All Truth and Majesty
Sacredness and Beauty
Of a Hidden Reality!

To Hear
To feel to Know
To Truly see what's Real
Can only come
to those who Seek
To such will
Heaven Reveal!

And when we gain
That Hidden Glimpse
Of all Beauty
here below
The Pineal
Like a Lighthouse
Its Sight on you bestow

The Secret

Is Beauty
Hidden from our Gaze?
Why do we Fail to See?
Connection has been Broken
Once Repaired
Again we See!

The Secret Is never far from Sight
very close for sure!
But very few will find it
Without Knocking
on Heavens Door

Eyes that do not See
Ears that do not Listen
Hearts that do not Feel
The Most Important Lesson!
Beauty all around you
Look Hear and Listen
To find Love is your Voyage
Love your Lifes Mission!
Then to You Revealed
All Majesty and Hidden Truth!
There you will find the Treasure
And your Long Lost Youth!

Exert yourself
Labor forth
If you wish to find the Kingdom!

when you then receive it
you will also
find your Freedom

Then as a Child
You will see
the many Gifts Bestowed
From your Heart All Gratitude
Once again unfold!

You then will See
You then will Hear
Your Heart will overflow!
With Joy and Love and Gratitude
For all you see below!

Imprisoned by the Mind

Minds filled
to bursting
Like Monkeys in a Tree
Who ensure
the Beauty
All around
We will Never See!

There is
no Space
for Presence
No place for
this moments Gift!
So find the Now
While you can
Life is over Swift!

The Straw Man
The Tin Man
The Lion
Held the Secret
Deep within!
Nothing is withheld
From those
The Journey Do Begin!

Conscious of our Being
Our Presence and "I AM"
We Seek within the Silence

To Find Heavens Plan
The Journey begins
But Never Ends!
Even through
Deaths Door!
Through Eternity
Our Soul
Will Seek
Our Home
for ever more!
To Voyage
Into the Depths
Of Being
Seeking Heavens Light
Where we Find
And Discover
Our True
And Hidden Sight.

No more
Ifs or Maybes
No more Hidden
From your Sight
You will find yourself
Waiting there
Standing in the Light!

Fear not
the journey
Your Rewards
At every turn!
Await you on the Path
The Path of No Return!

Once Upon a Stone!

Once upon a Stone
I searched its Hidden Light
I looked Hard
looked Long But no Beauty
came to Sight!?

I sat awhile still Longer
Gazing at heavy mass
But still
The Beauty
remained from View
I threw it in the Grass!

Stone it landed
near a Tree
Rolling slowly on
all at once
From it I spied
A Shining like the Sun!

I picked it up
Once again
Looked at it anew!
And there laying on my Hand
I saw its Colors True!

Whites Pinks
Yellow Golds
Silver tones

And Greens
Shining like the Sun
Nothing could compare
I Knew what I had done!

I had become
Completely Present
At one
with all around
Nothing was
Hidden from me
Saw the Light
Heard every Sound!

Impossible Life

In many far off Galaxies
No life can exist?
But look awhile Deeper
There is something
We have missed!?

Science and Theologies
Compares all Life
To Man!
But surely
Like The Creatures
of our Deep
Life on other
Planets can!

Wait a little longer
We all then will see
How even Light can Live!
Consciousness will come Alive
Our Hearts will Truly Give!

For all is Life!
Earth
Air water and the Sun
Consciousness Awakens
Life back to Earth has come!

Each of us
Identifies

With
Fleshy mass Disguise
But a
Divine and Godly Being
Is revealed at
its Demise!

The Energy
Within us
A Reflection of Stars so bright
Soon our Evolution
Will Transform all
Back into Light

And as Light
we will Travel
To Cosmos
Far and Wide
Meeting many Galactic
Entities
From each
and Every side!

A Reality
Not of this World
Awaits to come to View
Not Separate
But a Part of Me
And You!

By Bodies Form
And Bodies Mind
"I" "Me" and "Mine" kept in the Play!
But when Freed

from these Imposters
Reality will Stay!

What is this Reality
Of which he likes to Speak??
It's the Here the Now
It is the Peace we seek

The Happiness
The Love
The Unity of our Souls
To you
It can be Revealed
Before bodies decay
unfold!

The Insanity of the Mind

The Insanity of the Mind
the
"Me I and Mine"
Grasping Wanting
But seek within
only there
will you Find!
Over One Hundred
And Thirty Million Souls
Killed in Twentieth Century
By "Me" and "I" and "Mine"
Such Insanity of the Mind!
Free ourselves
From
Mental Forms
Of the Mind

Seek the Light of Presence
Life then we will Find!

Insanity of the Mind
Destruction of our Kind
Let us all be Free
From Insanity of the Mind!

Living Power

What is the Vital Energy?
This Forms a Paradox?
"No Batteries Are Included"
It says so on the Box!

What is the Source of Living Life?
Like the Plants do we Receive?
Or by the Living Energy
That makes the Sea recede?

Could it be
The Rays Above?
From Magnetic Energy Below?
Or is it given from Within
When Dreamless Sleep
we Go?

No Time

Psychological Time
A Figment of the Mind
This will Dissolve from you
When the Now
You Seek and Find!

For in the Now
No Time is present
It Disappears from View
No Past
No Future
To be Found
Now only!
no more "You"

For When
Intensely Present
Only Breath to be your Friend
The Un Manifested Invisible world
to you then will Attend!
When Invisible
made Visible
To you it is Exposed!
Experience then Enlightenment
This every Buddha Knows!

Creating Gaps

Creating Gaps
And Spaces
Between Incessant
Thoughts of Mind
Allows the Silence to Enter In
There Peace and Love You'll Find

How do you Create such Freedom?
From Monkey Minds Chatter?
By Breath
By Presence
Awareness and
Practicing all
the Latter!
Stop
the mental Commentary
Monkey Chatter
in your Head
Find the Truth
of
Every Poem
You have Read

Like Jesus and The Buddha

Like Jesus
And The Buddha
Enlightened You will be!
Free from all Attachments
And Beauty you will see!

Like Jesus and the Buddha
Your Light and Energy Know
Giving Healing to Yourself
Then to others it will Flow!

Like Jesus and the Buddha
Your Soul will long for Home
In Happiness and Peace
On Earth you will roam

Like Jesus and the Buddha
Your Heart will flow with Love
To all that live beside you
A Gift from up above
Like Jesus and the Buddha
Light within
your Core
Radiating
Sacred Healing
A Frequency So Pure!

Awaken

Continual Mind Activity
Imprisoned
By Endless Thought
Separates your Connection
From the Beauty you've
Always sought

A Wise man
Once he told me
Pay your thoughts no heed
"Make yourself Equanimeous"
From Thoughts
you will be Freed

The same Wise man
He told me
"let it go, it will pass"
But like a fool I ignored him
I let the years amass!

The Day I awoke
As if from a long dream
I understood the Wise man
No longer Mad
Did he seem!

I Awoke and Declared Freedom

From Lack
From Insufficiency
From Wanting
From Needing
From Grasping
From Compulsive Thinking
From Past and Future
From Time
From Incompleteness
From Attachments
I declared Freedom
from all Ego driven
Mind Agendas
I am Now
"Free from the Mind"

Being Love

A Holy man
Once spoke the words
"the greatest of these is Love"
"Love is Patient and Kind"
"Love does not Envy"
Love is not
of the Mind!

Love is not
self-seeking
Boastful or Envious
Love not
easily Angered
Does not
delight in Evil
Love protects Trusts Hopes
Perseveres and never Fails
Completeness is Love!

Not those who spoke like Angels, gave all they had to the Poor, only those in Possession of Love can enter the Higher Kingdoms Door!

Unique R U

Love doesn't make
One-person Special
It held in the Heart
for All!
When we become one
with being
We become one
with all!
Make no mistake!
My Love is for you
You are Special
Truly Unique
Accept my Acceptance of You
This is the Love that you Seek!

And when you Reflect that same Love
And Accept me just as I am
Then together forever we can be
United we'll chorus "we can"!

Say "Goodbye" to You

Give up
the attachment to You
The relationships
needed no more!
Once you Accept
your True being
You Enter
Enlightenments Door!

Through that Door
No Polarity or Duality
Is found waiting for you
Only Oneness
Unity
Connection
The all that is Loving and True!

Dissolving the Past, allowing the Present, a Miracle begins to transform, both within and without, a brilliant Light shines, a Light as Bright as the Dawn!

The Imposter called "Ego"

Power and Greed
Resistance Control
Defense and also
Attack!
These are the Weapons
of Ego's Domain
causing Heartache
Sadness and Lack!

If we could see
The much Misery
Of Ego's deliberate Dance
We'd see Exploitation
Death and Destruction
of Nations
And Never by Chance!

When Ego's come together
Dramas begin to Occur
Where Ergo is there will always be
The Characters of Lion and Bear!
Imagination Magic

Why not make Life Magic!
Bring to Life your Mind
Awaken Imagination
Where all your Dreams Unwind!

Bring to Life
All Ventures
Creations Large and Small
If you believe in Minds Magic
You get to Live
with them all!

Imagination is Magic
But Lost
when we grow Tall!
If we can bring back the Magic
for one
We bring back
the Magic for all!
"Become ye as a Little Child"

Daffodils

Through cold white Snow
Green shoots stood tall
With Tips of Sunny Bright Yellow
Reaching to the Sky Above
Becoming a Pretty Fellow

Golden Amber Petals
Unfurl a dazzling Garb
Only Splendid Tulip
Can be held in such regard!

Weather Near
Or Weather Far
The Daffodil stands Bright
All who pass them by
Utter
"what a LOVELY sight"!

Sunny yellow Dress, of such great majesty, gently waving in Spring
Green, warming Hearts, smile to Lips, Daffodil so Serene!

Apple Tree

Stopping to Admire
the Aging Apple Tree
Each time I pass it by
I feel it's Majesty

Stands in all The Seasons
Arms Held open wide
Outside of my Window
Ever by my side

Weather in the Snow or Sun
In Day or Night, I view
Smile comes to my Heart
I feel at one Not two!

Aging Tree
My old Friend
Even when apart
my fondness does not end
Your always in my Heart

A Young Prisoners Tale

"I have 4 voices in my Head"
The young Detainee said to me
"One is Female and very nice"
3 are Male who tell her
"with a Sharp Knife she can slice"!

The Older Male voices
in her head
Angry and severe
these voices speak to her
Leaving her in Fear!

Young Detainees Body
marked with many Scars
Old and fresh
Across her Throat
Now led to
Prison Bars!

Addiction gets her through
Each night
Music Drugs and Alcohol
often turns to Fight
The Voices Screaming to be Heard
above the self-made Hell
sends her running
to the Streets
Police carried her
where she fell!

The Swamp

He said a Swamp Existed
And he would clean it all!
In Washington DC
They began to Fall!

He began his Swampy Clean
With James Comey
`Head of FBI
Then Mueller and McCabe
For telling him a Lie!

But always in the background
Was Hillary and G Bush
Paying off in Millions
To keep the Deep State Hush!

Some wanted to Impeach Him
Declare him quite Insane
Others wanted his Death!
With a lot of Pain

The Corruption on the Hill
on a Scale never seen before
So it's time for them to go Now
He's showing them the Door!

Trey Gowdy from Carolina
wants to join the Fun

In Cleaning out the Swamp
Now the Rats are on the Run!

So who is on his side?
It's very hard to Know!
With all the Fake Media News
The Truth is very Slow!

Putin says "No It really wasn't us"
Put the blame on someone else
Stop making such a Fuss!

"Let's get down to Business"
"speak about Hillary on the Phone"
"Talk about hacked Emails,
make the Swamp Rats Known!

Loretta Lynch met Bill Clinton
Whilst sitting on Her Plane
He said it was "a Social Call"
just "sheltering
from the Rain!

Hillary Had her Meeting
With the King of Morocco
She said she would support him
If he gave her all his Dough!

Uma Aberdine
Is nowhere to be seen
last we heard she had been Sacked
Targeted by her Queen!

But Uma says she's Insured
With Information she has stashed!
Bill and Hillary's Charity Laundering
And "Favors" they have cashed!

Mr. Trump
"Please don't tarry"
Let's see the Swamp
Clean and Dry
lock them all up quickly,
before you say
"Goodbye"

The Event

The Event will come
With flash from Sun
All Hearts be Prepared

The Cosmos are ticking
It time for the Picking
Awakening has begun

Every Knee Shall Bow
each will know
Now hidden
Will be revealed

Don't be surprised
When we open our Eyes
To see a New Earth in View

In Earth's Atmosphere
All will Cheer
And
Humanity will
Be Free

A new Frequency
change you and Me
Light
will change
wrong to Right?
Hearts bright day

From night!
As TV's returning
The Light is Preparing
And all of the Dross
will be Gone

Prepare for Tomorrow
Release all your Sorrow
Our Children
Will Sing once again
We to Earth
Did choose this Time
When the Light
Of change would flow

Take a moment
connect
With the Birds Sky and Trees
all of your moments
reveal to you
How you Feel
and what you will do!
**Then you will see
All is my I and you are my Me!**

He Cried!

"The Bridge" he said
"but I was stopped from harm"
So "I tried again in Germany"
"Police they raised the alarm"

He sat on his Bed
knife to his side
Wife banging
Bedroom Door
She was just in time

I asked him "why be Dead"?
In tears he replied
"I want to Escape from all my Fears
And the Tears I Hide inside"

"What is it you fear most"?
He shook and sobbed some more
"I'm afraid of Everything
and want to Live no more"

Touching him gently
on the Shoulder
I spoke calm and Low
I told him
"that I cared for him"
His tears again did flow

He looked at me
And asked
"do you really care"?
Sincerely answered "yes I do"
"It could be me, sat crying in that chair"!

"Act the way you want to be, and soon, you'll be the way you act" (**Leonard Cohan. Poetry**)

Don't Strive after the Wind

Thanks for the Present Moment
Don't let it pass you by
Only Now is real!
See it before you Die!

Don't wait all your Life
to start Living
Live in this Present Right Now
Give Now Your full attention
Now will then show you How!

So grasp it
feel it
See it
and Hear
Don't look away to see
Your Now is Now!
Now a Companion
Will be!

No Resistance

Accept
With no Resistance
With Lightness the Here and Now
truly be Living your Life
Then the Now
you will Allow!

Watch
just like The Buddha
All as it passes by
Accept each new
And Now moment
Without ever having to try!

Be a Part of Everything
Let your judgements
Now Cease
Each moment
you'll have a New Friend
A friend you will know as
"My Peace"

Addictions

Life flows with Ease
When you choose
not to Appease
And Dependency on all Form
Has gone

Life will improve
to you all will come
that which you long for
Be Done

So come into Now
See how you fare
Feel the Peace and the Joy
Waiting there!

Let go Irritation Anger and Stress
See all negativity Dissolved
Live in the Light and Now will be Bright
All of your Issues resolved!

"Know ye Not that ye are Gods"?

When all is surrendered
When you become One
the Race
That you Started
You Won!

The Light grows Brighter
Within you Each Day
Your Now a Companion
With you to Stay!

When things go wrong
As they sometimes do
Let go of Resistance
Allow Now to do!

Surrender allows Positive
Energy to Flow
Where? What? And How?
You always will Know!
Rise far above and you will see Clearly the way!

No More Separation

When the Mass of Mankind
Open their Mind
To Loves Power Energy
All as One Live
Hearts want to Give
Unity Consciousness Synergy!

"Peace beyond understanding"
Joy and Love Reborn
Take back the Power
Truly Ours!
With Light
We are Being Reborn!

As the Rays of that Light Shine in Darkness
Frequency of Love will change all
Earth reside in its Peace
Redeemed forever from Fall!

No more Separation Divide us, no more the Ego Will Fool, no more Precious Souls Captured, fear no longer will Rule!

"My Father and your Father"

When Jesus said to Our Father
"Father, we will always be one"
Never be separated from you
Because "I am your Son"

We All
Are Sons and Daughters
Created in our Fathers Image
That same Power
ours to Command!
"Now is the Time and the hour"
To claim our True Lineage!

Declare Your Freedom from Mind
Let Ego no longer be Kings
Take back your Peace and your Power
Your oneness with all Living Things!

Whoever will say and "Believing"
"To all that we will command"
It "shall be done in that
Very Hour"
The return of DNA's Holy Strand!

"Know ye not that you are Gods"
"Sons of the Living Highest"
"Let not your Hearts Be Troubled"
"You are Gods" Descendants
Fly at Fathers Behest!

The Memory of Home
You've Forgotten
"Ask and you will receive"
Don't let the "World Ensnare you"
"From your Greatness"
It will Deceive!

Windows

I've looked through many Life Windows
Seen the Good and the Sad
A conclusion I reached
There is No Good
And No Bad!

Why declare such
a Statement?
Why would I say such a Thing?
Because Circumstances I've witnessed
Determine if People Cry
Or they Sing!

Walk in Shoes of another
Enter Pain of Their Heart
See clearly how Actions
Determined
By Circumstances right from the Start!

To avoid all that's Bad, tragic and Sad, just Learn to Live in the Now.
Let go of the Past, let Future unfold, the amazing Happens somehow!
Only the Best

Nothing can stop your progression
It's there from time you were born
So Enjoy all your Now
Be who you are
The Sun will Rise on your Dawn!

Look closely upon all your Moments
All senses aware and Alert
What you see will Truly amaze you
Re your Peace
You will be the Expert!

Don't take my word
Put all your Now to the Test
Like Magnet and Gravity to you
Will be Drawn
Only Good and the Best!

HE HEALED ME!

As a Nurse, I met Jim after being assigned to escort him to his Transport to Home, from the Surgical Department of a large General Hospital. My first impression was of a Small wiry slim man, healthy complexion, with shoulders back and an upright posture, age 80 something, silver hair, piercing deep Blue Eyes, with a disarming smile. He greeted me with that smile as I approached him, welcoming me into his space, right hand extended towards me, which I took and shook firmly but gently, I was aware he was many years older than I, but his returned grip was of strength and confidence, his eyes seemed to looking through mine into my Soul! Which fascinated my curious nature. I introduced myself "hi Jim, nice to meet you, with your permission I will be your Escort for the next hour"

He appeared to be appraising me, I became very aware of a strength behind that gaze, I felt instinctively Jim was a man of his word, intelligent and forthright, he replied "Thank you! Hope you don't mind me calling you that way? I had a good friend with the same name, and I rather like the name"! He still gently held on to my Hand, as I responded "not at all Jim, call me what you like, but not always to my face!" We both laughed, the ice had warmly been broken. I felt comfortable with Jim. This was one of the several rare occasions in my life, when I had met a stranger, feeling I had known them a lifetime!

"Ok, if you're ready Jim, I will get you to your transport" Jim took a look around him, and with a sigh, at the six bed Ward Bay where he had spent the last Two Weeks. He sat himself nimbly into the

Wheelchair I had provided for him (Hospital Policy), to get him from the Top floor to the Ground Floor Discharge Lounge. "Come on then, it's time for me to get back Home, been here too long already"! I wheeled the Chair about face pushing from behind, we made our way to the exit Door and to the Lift. We had got about several feet ahead, when a group of Three Male Patients in Dressing Gowns and Pajamas, stood between us and the Ward Double Doors. "Jim, we wanted to Thank you, and wish you every good wish". Jim shook each of their hands warmly, clasping theirs with both his hands, a beaming smile on his Face, I thought I noticed a Tear in the corner of his Eye!

By the time we were going through the Ward Doors to the Lifts facing, Jim had been approached by another Half Dozen Nurses and Patients, all saying "Thank you Jim"! I was very curious, no one had mentioned why they were Thanking Jim!? Whilst we were waiting for the Lift to arrive, I asked Jim "hope you don't mind me asking Jim, why were all those Patients and Nurses saying Thank you"? Jim simply said "I helped them" still curious I asked "how"? He looked at me, full eye contact and said "to get better"! Now, my curiosity was burning, I really wanted to know the meaning of what he was saying! The Lift arrived notifying us with a bell sound. Lift Doors opened, I pushed Jim in his Wheelchair forward into the small aluminum and mirrored surfaced interior, pressed Ground floor illuminated Button, and watch the Doors slide slowly shut. I couldn't help myself, I asked Jim "how did you help them to get better"?

He replied "I learned to do it whilst in the Services in Africa" by the time the Lift reached the Ground Floor, I had learned Jim was a serving SAS Officer in WW11 based in Africa, there he and 6 other Special Service personnel lived for 6 months, disguised as African Dessert Nomad Tribe members! They would secretly attack and destroy Ammunition and Fuel Dumps belonging to the German Forces stationed in Africa, then retreat back into the Dessert.

Jim told me, it was while living as a Tribe member, that he had been singled out by the Shaman Healer of the Tribe, who took Jim as a young man under his wing, teaching Jim the ways to Heal Other

Humans and Animals who were suffering. So, what Jim was telling me was "he had healed the Patients and Nurses who had thanked him! Wow! The monkeys in my mind immediately began to doubt, and question whether Jim may have Dementia or Alzheimer illness?

This doubt remained in my mind, right to where I had reached the Ground Floor Exit door to Jims waiting Transport. It was here that Jim put his foot down on the ground to stop the Wheelchair! "You ok Jim"? I asked! Jim looked up at me from the Chair and asked "would you let me heal your back"? Thoughts raced about my Mind, Alzheimer's Dementia? To "how did Jim know I was suffering with my back? I had hurt my back lifting a Patient several years before, I had learned to live with the constant and nagging daily pain, I had no limp, nor did I complain to anybody of my discomfort! Feeling embarrassed, work colleagues and others were about! I just wanted to say "goodbye Jim" but his eyes held me like a Rabbit in Headlights! Hesitantly, "oh go on then Jim, but hurry as your Transport is waiting"!

"Can you stand in front, with your back to me"? I did as Jim asked, feeling very self-conscious, now all eyes of Colleagues, discharged Patients and other Staff were on me and Jim! I was so shallow minded at that time; all I could think about was myself! With my back to Jim, I suddenly felt the heat from Jim's hands, which radiated deeply into my body, right at the very point of my historical and current discomfort!

"Right," he said kindly "all done, give it an hour or so and you will be fine"! This was crazy! Why did this old man think he could heal my back? But One hour later 2009 and to date 2018, I have not had discomfort from this Injury!?......... Three years later I headed to India to discover the Healing Energy of the Human Body.

King Queen Villain and Thief

When lives
Have all been written
Each of us will see
None were different
I am you
You are Me!

Many a guise
we starred in
the detail on every page
wanting to experience
Good bad and ugly
In Mankind's
every age

I
We
Me
You
In life
The" I" played
our Roles
Rich Poor
Saint and Witch
Screaming
In red hot coals!

One day
No more

lives to live
No more
deaths to die
No more
wars and hunger
No more
the children cry

The light
blazes bright once more
New heaven and Earth begun
Only love
abides this space
The "I"
Will live as one
We came
To Earth from Heaven
Clothed in flesh and blood
lives already written
No turning back
was understood!

You chose
your Earthly Parents
knew them
They were you!
you gave them
Free will and choice
To do what they would do.

No memory
Of our Earthly Plan
Remained as we arrived
We awoke in the Arms

of a Mother
A Mother we had contrived

One Mother
Sweet and loving
one vivacious and wild
we wanted
never to judge them
As we grew
From innocent child

We will go down
became mortal
physical life and insight
learn From each other
our oneness
one-day return
to the Light

After many
Incarnations
Deeds glorious cruel
some dread!
We'll become one forever with Universal Godhead!

Experiencing Your Awakening signs

Recalibration of DNA
leaving Third Dimension
Accelerated by
Rays above
Mind Body
Souls in tension

Symptoms noticed
Lifestyle, Sleeping patterns
Eating and choice of Friend
Body pains shoulders neck and spine
Nothing to Defend

Appearing Younger Healthier
Whilst feeling worn
and tired
Sensations of
Vibrational Ripples
by sight and touch acquired

Time is now unreal
retreat from
crowds and noise
Memories of Previous Lives
Makes you laugh
irritates and annoys

Awareness
Of Beauty and nature
Affection from
Birds and the Bees
Obsessions with Moon and the Sun
Oneness with skies and the Seas

Intuition tells me
Life beyond Earth
It exists!
Technology advanced
is well hidden
That Global Control
may persist!

Astronomy
Quantum Physics
Buried Secrets
Mankind needs to awake
To give them power
and knowledge
What "power over others"
Did take!

Electronic Equipment
Crashing and Glitching
Movements at corner of your eyes
Random memories of past life emotions
Of joy and happiness
Pass by!

Struggle
At everyday tasks
energy falls and you crash

What normally trigger the Fears
No longer emotions
So rash!

Demanding
Toxin Free Water
Food organic pesticide none!
Something Hidden is happening
Fake News lies
There is a change in the Sun!

Recognizing History's
been buried
re narrated written anew!
By those who
Want only Power
Over me
and taken from you!
Intuitions
Premonitions increased
Nausea Tinnitus Prolonged
Each will one day awaken
Put right
What has been wronged!